SEEING THINGS AS THEY ARE

SEEING THINGS AS THEY ARE

A Theory of Perception

John R. Searle

OXFORD
UNIVERSITY PRESS

OXFORD
UNIVERSITY PRESS

Oxford University Press is a department of the
University of Oxford. It furthers the University's objective
of excellence in research, scholarship, and education
by publishing worldwide.

Oxford   New York

Auckland   Cape Town   Dar es Salaam   Hong Kong   Karachi
Kuala Lumpur   Madrid   Melbourne   Mexico City   Nairobi
New Delhi   Shanghai   Taipei   Toronto

With offices in

Argentina   Austria   Brazil   Chile   Czech Republic   France   Greece
Guatemala   Hungary   Italy   Japan   Poland   Portugal   Singapore
South Korea   Switzerland   Thailand   Turkey   Ukraine   Vietnam

Oxford is a registered trade mark of Oxford University Press
in the UK and certain other countries.

Published in the United States of America by
Oxford University Press
198 Madison Avenue, New York, NY 10016

Library of Congress Cataloging-in-Publication Data
Searle, John R.
Seeing things as they are : a theory of perception / John R. Searle.
     pages   cm
Includes index.
ISBN 978-0-19-938515-7 (hardcover : alk. paper)
1. Perception (Philosophy)   I. Title.
B828.45.S425   2014
121'.34—dc23   2014007473

5 7 9 8 6

Printed in the United States of America
on acid-free paper

For Dagmar

CONTENTS

CONTENTS

ACKNOWLEDGMENTS

I want to thank all of the people who affected my production of this book: Ned Block, Tyler Burge, John Campbell, Jennifer Hudin, Jeff Kaplan, Mike Martin, John McDowell, and Umrao Sethi. For a relentless criticism of the intellectual content, I thank Klaus Strelau. Thanks also to my Research Assistants Mei Mei Yang, Nicole Badovinac, and Xia Hwang. Special thanks to Jennifer Hudin for the index. As usual my greatest debts are to my wife, Dagmar Searle, and I dedicate this book to her.

SEEING THINGS AS THEY ARE

Introduction

This book is about perception. Like most authors who write about this subject, I will concentrate on vision. And though I did not intend originally to produce such a book, in a large part it is a celebration of visual experience. Along with sex and great food and drink, visual experience is one of the major forms of pleasure and happiness in life. There are other such things we take for granted that are sources of enormous pleasure if we bother to think about them: free bodily movement and the power of speech, for example. Along with visual experience, we take all of these for granted and so do not appreciate them as much as we do other sources of intense sensory pleasures.

I want to begin by identifying the territory. Close your eyes and put your hand over your forehead, covering your eyes: you will stop seeing anything, but *your visual consciousness does not stop*. Though you do not see anything, nonetheless you have visual experiences which are *something like* seeing darkness with yellow patches. Of course you do not see darkness and yellow patches, because you do not see anything; but you still have visual consciousness. The area of visual consciousness is quite constrained: In my case, it extends, roughly speaking, from the top of my forehead down as low as my chin. I am here speaking about the phenomenology and not about the physiological forehead and chin. I am talking about how it seems to me consciously. But the area of my visual consciousness is limited in that, for example, I have no visual consciousness behind my head or under my feet. But I definitely have visual consciousness in front of my face even with my eyes closed. That conscious area I just identified I will call the "subjective visual field." Open your eyes and suddenly the subjective visual field is full, and the reason it is full is that you become visually aware of—that is, you literally see—the objective visual field: the objects and states of affairs around you. Much of this book is about the relationship between the subjective visual field and the objective visual field. The most important point I can make right now is: in the objective visual field everything is seen or can be seen, whereas in the subjective field nothing is seen nor can be seen.

Why write a whole book about perception? The relationship between perceptual experiences and the real world—of which vision is the most important type of experience—was a major preoccupation, one may even say *the* major preoccupation, of Western philosophy for the three centuries after Descartes. Up to the twentieth century, epistemology was the center of philosophy and the mistakes that defined the field continue right up to the present time. This book will attempt both to remove the mistakes and to present an alternative account to those I am familiar with, both traditional and contemporary. I hope to provide a more adequate account of the relationship between perceptual experience and the objects of our perceptions.

I want to say a little bit about how this book fits into my earlier work. After I published an intentionalistic account of perception in *Intentionality*,[1] I did not think I had much more to say about the subject. As far as I was concerned, perception seemed to me in pretty good shape. Austin refuted the Argument from Illusion,[2] which was the origin of the classical sense datum theory stretching back at least to the seventeenth century. Grice established a causal component in perception.[3] And I tried to

1. Searle, John R. *Intentionality: An Essay in the Philosophy of Mind.* Cambridge: Cambridge University Press, 1983. Chapter 2, 37–78.
2. Austin, J. L. *Sense and Sensibilia.* Oxford: Clarendon Press, 1962.
3. Grice, H. P. "The Causal Theory of Perception," in *Studies in the Way of Words.* Cambridge, MA: Harvard University Press, 1989. Chapter 15, 224–47.

explain the presentational intentionality of perception in ways that would enable us to see the logical structure of perceptual experiences. Such experiences, without being linguistic, present an entire state of affairs. They are causally self-reflexive. They are above all presentational rather than representational. (Please do not worry if you do not understand the jargon of causally self-reflexive, presentational, and representational. I explain all of these terms in due course.)

There were some unclarities and incompleteness in my account. For example, a persistent misunderstanding was that my account made perception too complicated for animals to grasp. But of course the claim is not that animals *think* all this high-level analysis, but that the analysis simply describes what is going on in their experience. When they perceive something, they actually perceive it only if the object perceived causes the very perception of it. As an analogy of this point: if I say knowledge is justified true belief that avoids the Gettier counterexamples and I say, "my dog knows that someone is at the door," I am not thereby committed to the view that the dog is *thinking*, "I have justified true belief that avoids the Gettier counterexamples." It is an old mistake to suppose that if animals can think, then they must be able to think that they are thinking. And it is an extension of that mistake to suppose that if animals have complex intentional structures in perception and action, then they must be able to think about the content of these complex intentional structures.

A second misunderstanding was that when I said that perception is causally self-referential, I might be saying that the perceptual experience performs some kind of a speech act of referring to itself. I intended nothing of the sort. The idea is that the conditions of satisfaction of perceptual experience require that the state of affairs perceived functions causally in producing the perceptual experience. So the conditions of satisfaction require reference to the experience itself. And in that sense the experience is causally self-referential. To avoid this misunderstanding I now use the expression "causally self-reflexive" instead of "causally self-referential," but I intend the two expressions to mean exactly the same thing.

There is another notational change in this work. In *Intentionality*,[4] I used the notation $S(p)$ as the general form of intentional states where the "S" marks the type of state and the "p" the propositional content. So the belief that it is raining would be represented as

Bel (it is raining)

One beauty of this is that it matches perfectly the structure of the speech act. So the assertion that it is raining has a structure $F(p)$ where the "F" marks the type of speech act, the illocutionary force, and the "p" the propositional content. The assertion is of the form:

Assert (it is raining)

The general principle I followed was to put the entire conditions of satisfaction inside the parenthesis. The causally self-referential case would include the causal component inside the parenthesis. The logical form can also be applied to a visual experience. Thus if I see that it is raining, this visual experience will have the form:

Vis Exp (it is raining, and the fact that it is raining causes this Vis Exp)

This way we get the causal self-referentiality inside the propositional content. If we follow the principle that all the conditions of satisfaction must be part of the propositional content, then this is the right way to do it. But it misled a lot of people into thinking that I am claiming that you see the causal relation. And of course you do not

4. Searle, John R. *Intentionality*.

see the causal relation, the causal relation is just an experienced condition on veridicality. I now prefer the notation:

Vis Exp (it is raining)
CSR

where the "CSR" captures the Causally Self-Reflexive character of the intentionality. Various people suggested this notation to me; I think the first was Kent Bach. The new notation is intended to mean exactly the same as the old notation, but I hope it avoids misunderstandings.

So, except for clearing up the misunderstandings, it seemed to me that once the specific forms of the intentionality of perception were understood, and once the presentational character was adequately grasped, my original objectives in presenting a theory of perception would have been achieved.

Other problems in gaining acceptance for an intentional account of perception derive not so much from defects in my presentation as from persistent mistakes that philosophers tend to make about the nature of intentionality itself. There are still confusions between the *content* of the intentional state and the *object* of the intentional state. If I believe that Obama is president, the *content* of my state is the proposition that Obama is president; but the *object* is Obama himself. Philosophers persistently suppose that "a propositional attitude" (a dreadfully muddled terminology) must be an attitude to a proposition. This is a systematic confusion between content and object. This confusion carries over to the intentionalistic analysis of perception. Some people suppose that when I say perception is intentional and has a propositional content, I am saying perception is an attitude to a proposition. Worse yet, they think a proposition must be an abstract entity like a number. This conception would have the result that on an intentionalistic account, we would really have no access to the real world. We would just be related to abstract entities. This conception runs exactly opposite to the whole account I am presenting, and I have to clear up some of these general mistakes about intentionality in the course of the discussion that follows.

This book is essentially a continuation of the line of analysis that I began in Chapter 2 of *Intentionality*, where I offered an intentionalistic analysis of perception. I think now I see a great many things I did not see when I wrote that book. Not just solutions to pre-existing problems, but problems that I was not then aware of. I think the account in *Intentionality* is completely correct as far as it goes, but it does not go as far as I want to go in this book.

I was originally provoked, if that is the right word, to undertake more work on perception by conversations with Ned Block and Tyler Burge, who urged me to undertake an investigation of something called "Disjunctivism" that they characterized as "weeds growing in your own garden here in Berkeley." I did become interested in this, and I benefitted from conversations with my Berkeley colleagues, especially with John Campbell and Michael Martin, in trying to understand Disjunctivism. It seemed to me that Disjunctivism was, in a sense, accepting the worst feature of the classical argument against Naïve Realism, even though Disjunctivism was designed to defend Naïve Realism.

Because this work relies on my earlier work, especially intentionality and consciousness, but also because I want it to be completely self-contained, I have added two short appendices to Chapter 1: one about intentionality and one about consciousness. Many of the confusions in contemporary philosophy of perception derive from the authors' lack of a clear conception of intentionality and a mistaken conception of consciousness. These mistakes are derived, at least in part, from our unfortunate philosophical tradition. These appendices are brief and they repeat material that I have expounded at greater length elsewhere. But I believe they result in a book that is entirely self-contained.

Once you have established the intentionality of perception and given a general characterization of its features, the investigation opens up a whole lot of problems. I criticize Disjunctivism more or less incidentally in Chapter 6. The main intellectual thrust of the book is in Chapters 4 and 5. I try to answer the question of how the raw phenomenology of perceptual experiences determines the intentional content of the experience. In Chapter 7 I consider examples of unconscious perception as well as other forms of unconscious cognition, and I try to answer the claim that consciousness does not really matter very much. The classical philosophical problems of perception—about skepticism and the various traditional theories of perception—are considered only at the end in Chapter 8. To me the most important chapters are 1, 2, 4, and 5.

Chapter 1

The Bad Argument

One of the Biggest Mistakes in Philosophy in the Past Several Centuries

I. A SMALL FALLACY AND A LARGE MISTAKE

Philosophy never completely overcomes its history, and many of the mistakes of the past are still with us. Indeed we lack a single word to name the variety of mistakes, errors, fallacies, confusions, incoherencies, inadequacies, nonsense, and just plain falsehoods that we have inherited. It is imprecise to call all of these "mistakes," but I lack a better word. I believe the worst mistake of all is the cluster of views known as Dualism, Materialism, Monism, Functionalism, Behaviorism, Idealism, the Identity Theory, etc. The idea these theories all have in common is that there is some special problem about the relation of the mind to the body, consciousness to the brain, and in their fixation on the illusion that there is a problem, philosophers have fastened onto different solutions to the problem. This mistake goes back to the Ancients, but it has received its most famous exposition by Descartes in the seventeenth century, and has continued right through to the present mistakes such as the contemporary Computational Theory of Mind, Functionalism, Property Dualism, Behaviorism, etc. The important thing to see is that all these apparently different and inconsistent views are in fact expressions of the same underlying mistake, which just to have a label I have called Conceptual Dualism.[1]

A mistake of nearly as great a magnitude overwhelmed our tradition in the seventeenth century and after, and it is the mistake of supposing that we never directly perceive objects and states of affairs in the world, but directly perceive only our subjective experiences. The mistake has many different names, among them Descartes, Locke, Berkeley, Leibniz, Spinoza, Hume, and Kant. After Kant it gets worse. Mill and Hegel, in spite of all their differences, would also have to be included. In this book, I expose this mistake and its disastrous consequences, but my main aim is not historical. I want to give a more accurate account of perception, and much of the interest of the account is in its effort to correct the mistakes that preceded it. I will start by giving a bare-bones account of what I think is a correct theory of perception and of the mistake I am alleging. Later on, in Chapter 3, I will fill in the details. Like most philosophers who write about the subject, I will concentrate on vision. I will say something about the other modalities in passing.

If you have normal vision and are in reasonably good light, and you look around you as you are reading this book, you are likely to see the following sort of things: if you are indoors, you might see the table on which the book rests and the chair in which you are sitting. Under normal circumstance, there will be other furniture as well as walls, windows, a ceiling, and the other elements of an indoor scene. If you are outdoors, the scene is likely to be much richer, as you might see trees, flowers, the sky, and perhaps houses and streets. I will begin by trying to describe obvious facts about this scene and your perceptions that occur in the scene. First, you are *directly* seeing objects and states of affairs, and these have an existence totally *independent* of your perception of them. The perception is *direct* in the sense that you do not perceive something else by way of which you

---

1. Searle, John R., *The Rediscovery of the Mind*. Cambridge, MA: MIT Press, 1992, 26ff.

perceive the scene. It is not like watching television or looking at a reflection in a mirror. The objects and states of affairs have an *independent* existence, in the sense that they exist independently of being experienced by us. If you close your eyes, the objects and states of affairs continue as before but the perception ceases. Furthermore, in seeing these objects and states of affairs, you have conscious visual experiences that go on in your head. Again, if you close your eyes, these visual experiences will cease even though the objects and states of affairs continue. So there are two distinct elements: the *ontologically objective* states of affairs that you directly perceive, and the *ontologically subjective* experiences of them. All of this you know before you ever start theorizing about perception.

As soon as you begin to theorize, you will notice a third feature in addition to the objective reality and the subjective experience: there must be a causal relation by which the objective reality causes the subjective experience. You do not need to know the details, but you do know that the light reflected off the objects hits your eyeballs and sets up a sequence of causal events that causes the perceptual experience. Another fascinating feature, one important for our investigation, is that if you try to describe the objective reality you see and then try to describe your subjective experience of seeing it, the two descriptions are pretty much the same, the same words in the same order. For example, describing the objective scene, you might say, "There is a blue book resting on a brown table." Describing your subjective visual experience, you might say "I see a blue book resting on a brown table." If you have studied some philosophy and have become epistemically hesitant, you might preface the description of the experience by saying, "I *seem* to see" instead of "I see." And because the scope of "seem" can be ambiguous, if you really want to be philosophically precise, you could say: "I am having a visual experience which is exactly as if I were seeing a blue book resting on a brown table." There is a deep reason why the description of the subjective experience has to be pretty much the same as the description of the objective reality: The subjective experience has a *content,* what philosophers call an intentional content, and the specification of the intentional content is the same as the description of the state of affairs that the intentional content presents you with. When vision is correctly doing its biological job, the description of the intentional content and the description of the state of affairs it presents has to be the same because a main biological function of perceptual experience is to give you knowledge about the real world. The identity of the description of the content of perception and the fact perceived in accurate perception is exactly like the identity of the description of the contents of true beliefs and the corresponding facts. The specification of the content of my belief that it is raining uses the same words in the same order as the description of the fact in the world that the belief represents: It is raining. (More about this later.)

II. DIGRESSION ABOUT INTENTIONALITY AND PHENOMENOLOGY

Before we go any further, I have to introduce a couple of technical terms. I have already used the word "intentional" in its technical sense. Intentionality is that feature of the mind by which it is directed *at* or *about* or *of* objects and states of affairs in the world. Hunger, thirst, beliefs, perceptual experiences, intentions, desires, hopes, and fears are all intentional because they are about something. States of undirected anxiety or nervousness are not intentional, at least in cases where the subject is just anxious or nervous without being anxious or nervous about anything in particular. Intentionality has no special connection with intending in the ordinary sense.[2] Intending to go for a walk, for example, is just one kind of intentionality among others.

2. If "intentionality" has no special connection with "intending," then why use this word? The answer is we got it from German-speaking philosophers, who in turn got it from the Latin, *intensio.* In German, "Intentionalität" does not sound at all like "Absicht," the word for intention.

Intentional states, such as beliefs and desires, can succeed or fail. If the belief succeeds, it is true; if the desire succeeds, it is satisfied. I will say that in general intentional states are satisfied or not satisfied and the content of the intentional state determines its *conditions of satisfaction*. The content of the belief that it is raining is satisfied if and only if it is raining. The content of my desire to drink a beer is satisfied if and only if I drink a beer.

Much of this book will be about the intentionality of perceptual experience. For those who are unfamiliar with the theory of intentionality, I have added Appendix A to this chapter, where I summarize the theory and explain the attendant jargon. If you are completely comfortable with the notions of propositional content, psychological mode, direction of fit, conditions of satisfaction, causal self-reflexivity, intentional causation, the Network of intentionality, and the Background capacities that enable intentionality to function, then you can skip the Appendix altogether. But if these notions seem mysterious or unclear to you, I advise you to read the Appendix before going any further. Also, because I make use of a theory of consciousness that I have developed elsewhere, I have added a short Appendix B to explain consciousness. A correct account of conscious perception requires a correct conception of consciousness in general, and in Appendix B I try to correct some outstanding mistakes about consciousness.

Another technical term that I sometimes use is *phenomenology* and the adjective *phenomenological*. Phenomenology just refers to the qualitative aspect of our conscious states, events, and processes. Wherever there is consciousness, there is phenomenology. When you are totally unconscious, there is no phenomenology. Often it is essential to describe the special features of conscious perception and I need the vocabulary of phenomenology to do that. The word *Phenomenology* is also used as a name of a philosophical movement. I will have very little to say about Phenomenology as a movement and a lot to say about phenomenology as a phenomenon.

III. DIRECT REALISM

The view of perception that I have stated, that we directly perceive objects and states of affairs, is often called "Direct Realism" and sometimes called "Naïve Realism." It is called "realism" because it says we do have perceptual access to the real world, and "direct" because it says that we do not first have to perceive something else by way of which we perceive the real world. It is often contrasted with Representative Realism, which says we perceive representations of the real world rather than the real objects themselves. It is sometimes called "Naïve Realism" because it ignores the sophisticated arguments to the effect that you can never really perceive the real world. I used to prefer the term "Naïve Realism," but recently it has come to be associated with a false theory called "Disjunctivism," so I will mostly stick to "Direct Realism." I will explain and discuss Disjunctivism in Chapter Six. The conscious visual experiences are sometimes called "sense data," though this term is even more dangerous than "Naïve Realism." And when the world is as it appears to be in my perceptual experience, the perception is said to be veridical. You will hear more of these dreadful expressions "Naïve" or "Direct Realism," "sense data," "intentionality," and "veridical" in what follows. (I will try to avoid the even more ghastly "falsidical.") Just to avoid confusion, I will follow a convention I used in *Intentionality*[3] and use "experience" and "perceptual experience" in a way that is neutral between the veridical and the non-veridical, and "perception" to describe veridical experience. Thus, at present, I have an experience, indeed a perceptual experience, of seeing a computer screen in front of me. Because there really is a computer screen and I really am seeing it, it is more than just an experience; it is a perception: I am actually *perceiving* the screen in front of me. (Sometimes in this book when I

3. Searle, John R., *Intentionality*.

am quoting Berkeley and Hume, I have to depart from this convention because they use "perception" in a way that does not carry the implication of veridicality.)

IV. OBJECTIVITY AND SUBJECTIVITY

One last terminological point. I have already used the distinction between ontological subjectivity and ontological objectivity, and I need to explain the distinction. The famous distinction between objective and subjective is ambiguous between an epistemic sense, where "epistemic" means having to do with knowledge, and an ontological sense, where "ontological" means having to do with existence. In the epistemic sense, the distinction between the objective and the subjective is between different types of *claims* (statements, assertions, beliefs, etc.): epistemically objective claims can be settled as matters of objective fact, the subjective are matters of subjective opinion. For example, the claim that van Gogh died in France is epistemically objective. Its truth or falsity can be settled as a matter of objective fact. The claim that van Gogh was a better painter than Gauguin is epistemically subjective; it is a matter of subjective evaluation. Underlying this *epistemic distinction* is an *ontological distinction* between modes of existence. Some entities—mountains, molecules and tectonic plates for example—have an existence independent of any experience. They are ontologically objective. But others—pains, tickles and itches, for example—exist only insofar as they are experienced by a human or animal subject. They are ontologically subjective. I cannot tell you how much confusion has been generated by the failure to distinguish between the epistemic and the ontological senses of the distinction between subjective and objective. I will say more about this later. Pains, as I just said, are ontologically subjective. "But are they epistemically subjective as well"? It is absolutely important to see that that question makes no sense. Only claims, statements, etc. can be epistemically subjective or objective. Often statements about ontologically subjective entities such as pains can be epistemically objective. "Pains can be alleviated by analgesics" is an epistemically objective statement about an ontologically subjective class of entities.

V. DIAGRAMS OF VISUAL PERCEPTION

To summarize this brief account, the veridical visual perceptual scene contains two distinct phenomena: an ontologically objective state of affairs in the world outside your head and an ontologically subjective visual experience of that state of affairs entirely inside your head. The former causes the latter, and the intentional content of the latter determines the former as its condition of satisfaction. When I say the objective state of affairs is directly perceived, I mean you do not have to first perceive something else by way of which, or by means of which, it is perceived. Your experience, to repeat, is not like seeing something on television or in a mirror.

Diagramatically, we can represent different aspects of the situation. In the first diagram we simply show how the ontologically objective object causes an ontologically subjective visual experience. In the second diagram, we add to that the intentionality of the visual experience. And in the third we have the case of the hallucination, the identical type of visual experience with its intentional content but with no intentional object. For the sake of total completeness and clarity, I am providing three pictures. The first one just shows that the object is causing a visual experience. And if you do not accept that an objectively existing object can cause ontologically subjective experiences, then there really is nothing more to be said because you cannot understand conscious perception. In the second one, I add the intentionality of

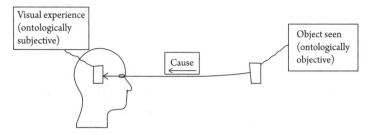

Figure 1.1. The box in the head represents the subjective visual experience caused by the object. The box outside represents the object perceived. I intend this picture to be philosophically uncontroversial.

the visual experience. The fact that the visual experience has intentionality is not agreed to by all philosophers, and I will defend it in the next chapter. So I devote a separate diagram adding the controversial intentionality to the non-controversial physical causation of visual experiences. With his eye, the subject receives stimulation from the object, which causes in him a visual experience. The object is ontologically objective. The visual experience is ontologically subjective. The visual experience itself has intentionality, and I represent that with an arrow that goes from the visual experience itself to the object.

The intentionality of visual experience requires defending in a way that the causal impact of the object on the visual system does not. The third shows how the same type of experience with its content can exist without the object.

The objects and events in visual perception are all parts of the real world and any theory of perception owes us such diagrams to give a systematic account of their relations. Conditions of adequacy on any such diagrams are that they must capture the ontological subjectivity of the perceptual experience, the ontological objectivity of the state of affairs seen, and the causal and other relations between them. Because the elements of the perceptual situation, including the ontologically subjective experiences, are really existing objects, events, and states of affairs in the world,

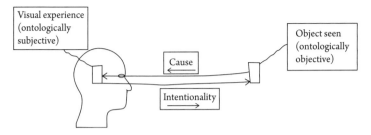

Figure 1.2. The upper line represents the causation by which the objective box causes the subjective experience. The direction of causation is from world-to-mind and the direction of fit of the intentionality is from mind-to-world. This figure adds a lower line that represents the intentionality of the experience, which presents the object as its conditions of satisfaction. This figure contains the controversial claim that the visual experience has intentionality.

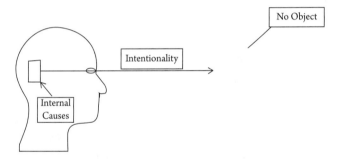

Figure 1.3. Hallucination. The internal processes in the brain are sufficient to produce a visual experience which is type identical with the visual experience produced by the external stimulus. The visual experience has the same intentional *content* as the veridical experience, but there is no *object* of the visual experience.

any theory of perception ought to be able to present a diagram of their relations. Real events in the real world have to be representable diagrammatically. Anyone objecting to my account owes us an alternative diagram.

I believe these diagrams are accurate, but they can be dangerously misleading if they suggest that the internal visual experience is itself an object of perception. Supposing that the internal experiences are themselves objects of perception is one of the major mistakes that this book aims to overcome. The subjective visual experience cannot itself be seen, because it is itself the seeing of anything.

Actually, I hope the account so far seems obvious to the point that you wonder why I am boring you with these platitudes. But here is the amazing thing: The account I just gave you is denied by just about every famous philosopher who writes on this subject. Indeed of the philosophers that have written about perception since the seventeenth century, I do not know of any Great Philosopher who even accepted Naïve or Direct Realism. ("Great Philosophers" in this period begin with Bacon and Descartes and end with Kant. They include Locke, Leibniz, Spinoza, Berkeley, Bacon and Hume. If someone wants to count Mill and Hegel as Great Philosophers, I will not argue the point.)[4]

VI. THE ARGUMENT FOR THE REJECTION OF NAÏVE, DIRECT REALISM

Why would anyone in his or her right mind want to reject Direct Realism? There are a number of different arguments against Direct Realism, but oddly enough all those known to me rest on exactly the same mistake. I now want to expose that mistake because it is the central mistake of modern epistemology. It is the single greatest disaster from which all the little disasters follow, as we will see. Here is how the Bad Argument in its simplest form goes:

---

4. I specify these philosophers because I once wrote that none of the *Great Philosophers* in the past had a theory of speech acts, and somebody "refuted" me by citing a German I had, at that time, never heard of, Alfred Reinach, who wrote in the early part of the twentieth century. Maybe my critics count Reinach in the same category as Kant, Leibniz, Hegel, Descartes, Berkeley, Spinoza, and Hume, but I do not. In this footnote I want to make clear who counts as a "Great Philosopher," and I do so by providing the list above.

In the scene, I imagined you were seeing the table with a book on it and the surrounding accoutrements. But suppose that you were having a hallucination. Suppose that the whole scene did not exist in reality, but you were having a hallucinatory visual experience indistinguishable from seeing such a reality. The perception in the hallucinatory case was not veridical, but all the same in this case you were still *conscious of something.* Indeed you were *aware of something,* and we could even say—though we might have to put sneer quotes around "see" when we say it—you did *see something.*

Here comes the next step. By hypothesis, the experience in the hallucinatory case is indistinguishable from the experience in the veridical case. So if we are going to be consistent, whatever we say about the hallucinatory case, we have to say the same thing about the veridical case. In the hallucinatory case you did not see a material object, but you did see something. We need a name for these "somethings." In the works of Descartes, Locke, and Berkeley, they are called "ideas." In Hume they are called "impressions." In the twentieth century they came to be called "sense data."

The conclusion is obvious. You never see material objects or other ontologically objective phenomena, at least not directly, but only see sense data. This argument in various forms is called "The Argument from Illusion." If you accept its conclusion, then the question for epistemology is: What is the relation between the sense data that you do see and the material objects that apparently you do not see? Different answers to this question define modern epistemology. According to Descartes and Locke, the sense data, in certain respects, resemble the material objects. They resemble the primary qualities and so we can get information about the primary qualities of the objects from perceiving the sense data. The sense data are representations of the objects, so this theory is sometimes called the "Representative Theory of Perception" or "Representative Realism." According to the Phenomenalists and the Idealists—such as Berkeley—the objects just are collections of sense data. The only things that exist, says Berkeley, are minds and ideas in the minds. According to Kant, all we can perceive are representations; but in order to guarantee epistemic objectivity, Kant claims that there have to be things in themselves that are the ground (Grund) of the representations. Things in themselves are unknowable. This view is called "Transcendental Idealism."

A modern version of this argument that is superficially different but rests on the same fallacy is called "the Argument from Science." Here is how it goes: A scientific account of perception shows that our perceptions are entirely caused by a sequence of neurobiological processes that begin with the stimulation of the photoreceptor cells in the retina by photons reflected off objects in the world. The activation of the photoreceptor cells sets up a series of neurobiological processes that eventually ends in the cortex in a visual image. In common sense talk we say that we see the table, but when we give a real scientific analysis we have to conclude that all we can see is the visual image or sense datum. Science shows that we never see the real world but see only a series of events that are the result of the impact of the real world, by way of light reflectances, on our nervous system. Once again Direct Realism is refuted.

In order to show how all of these arguments rest on the same fallacy, I need to state the argument as a series of steps. I will do this for the Argument from Illusion.

> Step One. In both the veridical (good) case and in the hallucination (bad) case, there is a common element—a qualitative subjective experience going on in the visual system.
> Step Two: Because the common element is qualitatively identical in the two cases, whatever analysis we give of one, we must give of the other.
> Step Three: In both the veridical case and the hallucination case we are aware of something (are conscious of something, see something).

Step Four: But in the hallucination case it cannot be a material object; therefore, it must be a subjective mental entity. Just to have a name, call it a "sense datum."

Step Five: But by step two we have to give the same analysis for both cases. So in the veridical case, as in the hallucination, we see only sense data.

Step Six: Because in both hallucinations and in veridical perceptions themselves we see only sense data, then we have to conclude that we never see material objects or other ontologically objective phenomena. So Direct Realism is refuted.

This basic argument in many different forms was the foundation of modern epistemology, where "modern" means from the seventeenth century on. I have claimed rather briskly that it had disastrous consequences. Why? Notice that the only reality that is accessible to us on this account is the subjective reality of our own private experiences. This makes it impossible to solve the skeptical problem: How, on the basis of perception, can we ever know facts about the real world? The problem is insoluble because our only perceptual access is to private subjective experiences, and there is no way to get from the ontologically subjective experiences to the ontologically objective real world. Hume had the sense to see that skepticism became inevitable, but he thought that our intellectual laziness would enable us to simply ignore the skeptical results and go on as if nothing had happened. Hume thought that all we could ever perceive are our own private experiences, "impressions" in his jargon, but that nonetheless we believe that these are objects and therefore have both a continuous existence—"continuous" even when we are not perceiving them—and a distinct existence—"distinct" from our perception of them. Hume thought the belief in a continuous and distinct existence of objects of perception was ridiculous, but we could not help holding such beliefs. Hume indeed thought that Direct Realism was so obviously false that he only bothers to refute it in a couple of sentences. If you are tempted to Direct Realism, he tells us, then just push one eyeball. If Direct Realism were true, then the world would double. But it does not double. The only thing that doubles is our sense data or impressions.[5] I will criticize his argument in detail in Chapter 3.

VII. THE FALLACY IN THE ARGUMENT

I now want to expose the fallacy in the argument. One could object to various steps, but the crucial step is number three, which says that in both the hallucination and the veridical case we are "aware of" or "conscious of" *something.* But this claim is ambiguous because it contains two senses of "aware of," which I will call respectively the "aware of" of intentionality and the "aware of" of constitution. You can see the difference if you contrast two common-sense claims. First, when I push my hand hard against this table, I am aware of the table. And second, when I push my hand hard against this table, I am aware of a painful sensation in my hand.

    (a) I am aware of the table.
    (b) I am aware of a painful sensation in my hand.

Both of these are true and though they look similar, they are radically different. (a) describes an intentional relation between me and the table. I had a sensation where the table was its intentional object. The presence and features of the table are the conditions of satisfaction of the sensation. In (a) the "aware of" is the "aware of" of intentionality. But in (b) the only thing I am aware of is the painful sensation itself.

5. Hume, David. *A Treatise of Human Nature,* ed. L.A. Selby-Bigge. Oxford: Oxford University Press, 1888, 210–11.

Here the "aware of" is the "aware of" of identity or the constitution of the experience. The object I am aware of and the sensation are identical. I had only one sensation: a painful sensation of the table. I was aware of (in the sense of identity or constitution) the sensation, but I was also aware of (in the sense of intentionality) the table.

Applying this lesson to the Argument from Illusion, we get the following result. In the case of the veridical perception I am literally aware of the green table, nothing more. But what about the hallucination? In the sense in which I am aware of the green table in the veridical perception, in the case of the hallucination, *I am not aware of anything.* In the ordinary sense, when you are having a total hallucination, you do not see anything, you are not aware *of* anything, you are not conscious *of* anything. But the source of the confusion is the following: In such a case you are having a conscious perceptual experience, and ordinary language allows us to use a noun phrase to describe that experience and to treat that noun phrase as the direct object of "aware of." In that sense I am aware of a visual experience, but this is a totally different sense from the intentionalistic sense because, to repeat, the visual experience is identical with the awareness itself; it is not a separate object of awareness. In the case of the hallucination, there was an intentional content but no intentional object; there was an intentional state where the conditions of satisfaction were not satisfied.

At the most fundamental level the entire argument rests on a pun, a simple fallacy of ambiguity, over the use of the English expressions "aware of" and "conscious of." The proof that the same expression is being used with two different senses is that the semantics is different. Consider sentences of the form: "Subject S has an awareness A of object O." In the intentionality sense, that has the consequence: A is not identical with O. $A \neq O$. In the intentionality sense: A is an ontologically subjective event that presents the existence and features of O as its conditions of satisfaction. But in the constitution or identity sense: A is identical with O. *The thing that one is "aware of" is the awareness itself* $(A = O)$.

Strictly speaking, the Argument from Illusion rests on a fallacy of ambiguity. But it would be misleading if I give the reader the impression that that is an ambiguity like the ambiguity in the word "bank" in "I went to the bank," which can mean either "I went to a finance house" or "I went to the side of the river." The ambiguity in "aware of" and "conscious of" is not at all like that. They are not two different dictionary meanings, as there are for "bank," rather because there is a common phenomenon to both the hallucination and the veridical perception. The temptation is to treat the visual experience itself as the object of the visual experience in the case of the hallucination, but in fact there is no such object. English and other European languages allow us to make this mistake because we can always invent an internal accusative for the verb phrase. It is a good example of Wittgenstein's claim that philosophical problems typically arise when we misunderstand the logic of our language. But the example is not an example of lexical ambiguity. The linguists' test of conjunction reduction shows this: "I am aware of the table" and "I am aware of a sensation in my hand" imply "I am aware of both the table and the sensation in my hand."

The reason we feel an urge to put sneer quotes around "see" when we describe hallucinatory "seeing" is that, in the sense of intentionality, in such cases we do not see anything. If I am having a visual hallucination of the book on the table, then literally I do not see anything. Since I am "aware of" something, the temptation is to put in a noun phrase to form the direct object of "see." We compound the ambiguity of "aware of" by introducing an ambiguity of "see." This shift from describing the ontologically objective state of affairs in the world to describing the ontologically subjective conscious intentional state itself underlies the whole epistemological tradition. The mistake derives from a failure to understand the intentionality of conscious perceptual experience. How exactly? There is obviously something in common between the veridical perception and the indistinguishable hallucination. They are, after all, indistinguishable.

If you fail to see that the something in common is a conscious intentional experience with conditions of satisfaction, you are likely to think that the something in common is itself the object of perception. That is, if you fail to understand the intentionality of the *experience*, you are likely to think the experience is the *object of the experience* in the hallucinatory case. In the diagram the hallucination is shown with the same type of visual experience and the same intentional content, but no intentional object and only internal causes. This shift is to move from the object-directed intentionality of the perceptual experience to treating the visual experience itself as the object of visual consciousness. I do indeed have a conscious experience when I see the table, but the conscious experience is *of* the table. The conscious experience is also an entity, but it is not the object of perception; it is indeed the experience itself of perceiving.

The Bad Argument is an instance of a very general fallacy about intentionality, and it results from confusion about the very nature of intentionality. It is a confusion between the *content* of an intentional state and the *object* of the intentional state. In the case of a hallucination, the visual experience has a content, indeed it can have exactly the same content as the veridical experience, but there is no object. The assumption that some authors make is that every intentional state must have an object, but this is confusion between the true claim that every intentional state must have a content and the false claim that every intentional state must have an object. It is just false that all intentional states have objects. Some authors even postulate an "intentional object" as a special kind of object for unsatisfied intentional states. So, for example, if the child believes his father comes home in the evening, the intentional object of his belief is his father. If he believes Santa Claus comes on Christmas Eve, his belief has no intentional object; it has a content but no object. Some philosophers find that uncomfortable and so they say there is a special kind of intentional object for intentional states about nonexistent entities.

I hope it is obvious that this is a confusion. In any case it is a confusion we will observe later on. Right now I just want to emphasize the Bad Argument does not stand alone; it is an instance of a more general confusion between content and object.

The reader familiar with the long history of the Argument from Illusion can go through the various steps and see the same fallacy being repeated over and over with such famous examples as the bent stick, the elliptical coin, and Macbeth's dagger. In every example the argument confuses the consciousness or awareness of the experience itself with its intentional content, on the one hand, and the experience of the object in the world, at which the intentional content is directed, on the other hand. However, just to show that I am not bluffing, in Chapter 3, I will go through a set piece (and possibly boring) five-finger exercise of showing how the same fallacy afflicts the traditional arguments for the claim that all we perceive are sense data.

It is not so obvious that the Argument from Science commits the same fallacy, so I will spell it out. Vision Science seeks an answer to the question: How do external stimuli cause conscious visual experiences? And the answer is given by a detailed analysis of the mechanisms that begin at the photoreceptor cells and continue right through the cortex. The answer is that these processes terminate in the production of a conscious experience, which is realized right there in the brain. But then it looks like the visual experience is the only object that the subject can be aware of, that he can perceive. But this is the same fallacy: the intentionality of the visual experience enables the experience to be an experience of objects and states of affairs in the world; but in the sense of "aware of," in which the subject is aware of the experience, the experience and the awareness are identical. In the intentionality sense of "aware of" the subject is at the same time aware of objects and states of affairs in the world. There is one experience, it has objects and states of affairs in the world as its conditions of satisfaction. And one can be both "aware of" (in the

constitutive sense) the experience and "aware of"(in the intentionality sense) the ontologically objective objects and states of affairs in
the world that the experience presents as its intentional conditions
of satisfaction. One experience, two senses of "aware of."

In what follows, by the expression "Bad Argument" I will mean
any argument that attempts to treat the perceptual experience as an
actual or possible object of experience. And I will also use the expression to name the conclusion of the argument, that one never sees
material objects directly. I have to say "actual or possible" because the
Disjunctivists, who accept the validity of the argument, dispute the
first premise. So they think that a sense datum is a possible object of
experience, but in the case of veridical perception it is not actual.

VIII. HISTORICAL CONSEQUENCES
OF THE BAD ARGUMENT

I said the denial of Direct Realism was disastrous and I want now
briefly to say how. The whole epistemic tradition was based on the
false premise that we can never perceive the real world directly. It is as
if one tried to develop mathematics on the premise that numbers do
not exist. After Descartes, the central problems of philosophy were
epistemic. In Locke's phrase, they were about "the nature and extent
of human knowledge." But if you deny Direct Realism, you can never
directly perceive objects and states of affairs in the world; how then is
it possible to get knowledge of facts in the world? The answers given
by Descartes and Locke are that our perceptions of the world, our
ideas, give us a picture of how things are in the world. It is as if we
were forever watching a movie but could not get outside the movie
house. We get knowledge of the world because in some respects the
pictures resemble the things they are pictures of. Our ideas of the primary qualities, which Locke lists as "solidity, extension, figure, motion

or rest and number"[6] actually resemble the primary qualities of the object. But our ideas of secondary qualities—color, sound, taste and smell—do not resemble actual features of the objects, but rather the ideas are themselves caused by the behavior of the primary qualities of the object. There are a number of things wrong with this view, but Berkeley pointed out the worst: it makes no sense to say that two entities visually resemble each other if one is completely invisible. The form of representation in question requires resemblance, but the resemblance in question is impossible because one term of the resembling relation is imperceptible to vision or any other sense. So there is no sense to the notion of representation. Ideas cannot look like objects because objects are invisible. As Berkeley says, "an idea can be like nothing but an idea."[7] (More about this in Chapter 8.)

Having made this decisive objection, one might wish that Berkeley would have gone back to Direct Realism. But he thought that the Argument from Illusion, of which he advanced several versions, refuted any version of Naïve or Direct Realism. So he came up with the theory that the only things that exist are minds and ideas. All ontological objectivity reduces to subjectivity. Objects just are collections of ideas. Epistemic objectivity, according to Berkeley, is guaranteed by God. We can have objective knowledge that there is a tree in the quad even when we are not looking at it because God is always perceiving the tree in the quad.[8] Hume did not share Berkeley's

---

6. Locke, John. *An Essay Concerning Human Understanding.* London: Routledge, 1894, 84.

7. Berkeley, George. "A Treatise Concerning the Principles of Human Knowledge." *A New Theory of Vision and Other Writings,* London: J.M. Dent & Sons, and New York: E.P. Dutton, 1910, Section VIII, 116.

8. There is a schoolboy limerick that summarizes Berkeley's philosophy for beginning philosophy students. It is much loved by philosophy lecturers, though I suspect it may bore their students:

There was a young man who said, "God
Must think it exceedingly odd
To think that this tree
Continues to be,
When there's no one about in the quad."

religious views, but he thought Berkeley was right in thinking that objects just are ideas in the mind, "impressions" in Hume's terminology. But though Hume thinks this view is correct, we find it unbelievable. We persist in thinking that objects have an existence independent of our experiences and continuous even when they are not being experienced. Hume explains how we make this mistake: we think we see objects like chairs and tables, but our only perceptual objects are impressions. But because we think chairs and tables have a continuous and distinct existence, we end up with the ridiculous view that impressions have a continuous and distinct existence. Hume thinks that there is no merit to the view that objects have a continuous and distinct existence, but we cannot help holding this view. Kant agrees with everybody that all we can perceive are our own subjective experiences—"representations," he called them—but he thought epistemically objective knowledge was possible because underlying our representations, and providing their ground, is a world of *things in themselves* which are unknowable.

If you think that I am overestimating the consequences of the rejection of Direct Realism, then try to imagine what the history of philosophy would have been like if the Great Philosophers had all been Direct Realists. For example, imagine Kant's *Critique of Pure Reason* rewritten on the assumption that we have direct perception and knowledge of things in themselves. I am not going to undertake such a rewriting, but I do think when things are going well we do have direct perception of things in themselves, and in this book I am working out some of the consequences of that assumption. Western epistemology

And then comes the reply;
"Dear Sir, your astonishment's odd.
I am always about in the quad,
And that's why the tree
Will continue to be,
Since observed by, Yours Faithfully, God."

has in large part gone around and around these mistakes for the past few centuries. I am going to argue that we cut through all the mistakes by rejecting the arguments against Direct Realism, and by accepting an intentionalistic account of perception that has Direct Realism as a consequence. In the next chapter I will set out such an intentionalistic theory of perception. This chapter has been brief, but I will spell its arguments out in more detail in Chapter 3 after I have explained the intentionality of perception.

Summary of the Theory of Intentionality

Many of the mistakes in the philosophy of perception stem from a failure to understand the specific intentionality of perceptual experience. And this failure in turn often comes from a failure to understand the nature of intentionality in general. This appendix provides a brief summary of the theory of intentionality and points out some of the most common mistakes people make about intentionality. For a more thorough presentation of my views, see *Intentionality* (1983).[1]

Intentionality is that feature of the mind by which it is directed *at*, or *about*, or *of* objects and states of affairs in the world. Intentionality is, above all, a biological phenomenon common to humans and certain other animals. The most basic forms of intentionality are the biologically primitive forms such as conscious perception, intentional action, hunger, thirst, and such emotions as anger, lust, and fear. Derivative forms are such things as belief, desire, and hope. To have a shorthand term, I use "intentional state" as a general term for all forms of intentionality, though, strictly speaking, many of them are not states at all but events, processes, and dispositions. Every intentional state consists of a *content* and a psychological *mode*. If I *see*

1. Searle, John R. *Intentionality: An Essay in the Philosophy of Mind.* Cambridge: Cambridge University Press, 1983.

that it is raining and I also *think* that it is raining, the two intentional phenomena, seeing and thinking, share a common content that it is raining. But the psychological modes, seeing and thinking, are clearly different in the two cases.

It is important to emphasize the *biological* character of intentionality. Many philosophers think there is some deep mystery about how anything in the brain can be *about* anything in the world outside the brain. This mystery is dispelled if we concentrate our attention on such simple animal feelings such as hunger and thirst. These are basic forms of intentionality. All intentional states, without exception, are *caused by* brain processes and *realized in* the brain. The alleged mystery of intentionality is like earlier mysteries that had a biological solution, such as the problem of life and consciousness. How can inert matter be alive? How can brains be conscious? As the problem of life is now seen as a biological problem—vitalism is out of the question—so I believe the problems of consciousness and intentionality are also biological problems—metaphysical dualism is out of the question—even though the details of the solutions to the problems are by no means obvious to us now.

The most philosophically interesting intentional states have entire propositions as contents. For example, beliefs and desires always have entire propositions as contents, even though this is sometimes disguised from us in the surface form of the sentence that reports the intentional state. If I say, "I want your house," that looks like it is just directed at an object. But in fact it has an entire propositional content, it means something like *I want that I have your house.* The proof of this is that statements of the form "I want x" take modifiers that make sense only on the assumption that there is concealed propositional content. Thus "I want your house next summer," means something like "I want that I have your house next summer." Any statement of wanting or desire will take such modifiers, and that proves that they are all intelligible only on the assumption of a propositional content. States that have entire propositions as contents are often called "propositional attitudes." This is a disastrous terminology because it suggests the false view that the intentional state is an attitude to a proposition. Nothing could be further from the truth. More about this later.

In using the concept of intentionality, it is absolutely essential to be clear about the distinction between content and object. Many of the mistaken theories of perception are based on a failure to make the distinction for perceptual experiences. For example, if I see a man in front of me, the content is *that there is a man in front of me*. The object is *the man himself*. If I am having a corresponding hallucination, the perceptual experience has a content, but no object. The content can be exactly the same in the two cases, but the presence of a content does not imply the presence of an object. The Bad Argument is a systematic manifestation of the confusion between content and object. The visual experience, which determines the content of my perception, is treated as the object of the perception.

Intentional states typically fit the world with one of two directions of fit. Perceptions, beliefs, and event memories are supposed to fit how a world is. They have the mind-to-world direction of fit. Desires and intentions are not supposed to fit how the world is, but how we would like it to be or how we intend to make it to be. They have the world-to-mind direction of fit. I think in simple metaphors. So I think of the mind-to-world direction of fit as an arrow pointing downward from the mind to the world ($\downarrow$) and the world-to-mind direction of fit as an arrow pointing upward from the world to the mind ($\uparrow$). Wherever an intentional state has an entire propositional content and a direction of fit, it will either match or fail to match the world. And I say in such cases that the intentional state is satisfied or not satisfied. So *satisfaction* is a general notion, of which *truth* is a special case. The key to understanding intentionality is *conditions of satisfaction*. Every intentional state that has an entire propositional content and a direction of fit is a representation (or presentation) of its conditions of satisfaction.

As biological phenomena, intentional states function causally in our very existence. Some have causal conditions built into their very intentional structure. So a *prior* intention to perform an action is satisfied only if the intention causes the agent to do the thing he intends to do. And a perceptual experience is satisfied only if the state of affairs perceived causes the perceptual experience. In both cases the causation is part of the conditions of satisfaction. I call such intentional phenomena "causally self-reflexive"[2] because the state itself, as part of its conditions of satisfaction, requires a causal role for the state. Perceptual experience and intentions to perform actions both are causally self-reflexive. But they have different directions of fit and different directions of causation. In the case of perception, the direction of fit is mind-to-world and the direction of causation is world-to-mind. In the case of intention, the direction of fit is world-to-mind and the direction of causation is mind-to-world. All of this is depicted on the accompanying chart.

Intentional states, such as beliefs and desires, almost never come in isolation. So if I, for example, believe that Obama is president, I must have many other beliefs in order to make sense of that belief. I must believe the United States has a government, that it is a republic, that there are presidential elections to elect the leader of the government, that the president is head of the executive branch of the government, etc. I use the expression *Network* to say that intentional states only function, only determine their conditions of satisfaction, within a Network of intentional states. This is certainly true of perception. I now see a tree in front of me that I know is a California

---

2. Originally I called them "causally self-referential." This terminology was misleading to some people who thought I was claiming that the state performs a speech act referring to itself. So to avoid this misunderstanding I prefer "causally self-reflexive."

Coastal Redwood, and I literally see that it is such a tree. But in order to see that, I have to have collateral information, and this is all part of the Network. In addition to the Network there is a certain set of Background abilities against which the intentionality functions. So if I intend to go skiing, I must also have a set of Background abilities and capacities—the ability to ski and the capacity to make my way to the ski resort, etc.

In the case of perception there are complex relations between the phenomenology and the intentional content. For the most basic cases, such as seeing the color red or feeling the smoothness of the table, the phenomenology entirely fixes the intentional content. But often a change in intentionality will produce a change in the phenomenology. If I believe that the object I am seeing is a house, it will look different from what it looks like if I believe it is only the façade of a house, even if the optical stimulus is the same in both cases. If I believe the car I am looking at is *my* car, it will look different to me from type identical cars made in the same year by the same manufacturer.

Here are ten or so common, but grave, mistakes to avoid. I have to mention all of them because I found all of them in my experiences of dealing with the intentionality of perception.

1. CONTENT AND OBJECT

The most important mistake to avoid is the confusion of content and object. Two perceptual experiences can have type-identical contents, but one has an object and the other one does not. This, as I have said, is true of the perception of an object and the corresponding hallucination. The perception is satisfied; the hallucination is not satisfied. They can have exactly the same content, but have an object in one case and not in the other case.

2. INTENTIONAL OBJECTS

A very common mistake, related to the mistake of confusing content and object, is that every intentional state has an intentional object. In the case of beliefs about nonexistent objects, there is nonetheless an object that has a kind of existence—what Brentano calls "intentional inexistence"[3]—and these intentional objects, objects of intentional states, are not to be thought of as actual objects in the world, but rather as objects in our mind when we have a belief. And those objects exist in the mind whether or not there is a corresponding object in the real world. This is another disastrous mistake because it prevents us from seeing that actual beliefs do indeed have intentional objects, when there actually is such an object in the world. So if I believe that Obama is president, the intentional object of my belief is Obama himself, not some mental entity. But what about the child's belief that Santa Claus comes on Christmas Eve? In such a case, *there is no intentional object.* The belief does indeed have a *content,* but no *object.*

3. PROPOSITIONAL ATTITUDES

According to the standard and mistaken view, an intentional state is a relationship between an agent and a mental representation (typically a proposition). So for example, if I believe that Obama is president of the United States, on this mistaken view I stand in a relation of believing to the proposition that Obama is president of the United States. This is why these sorts of states are called "propositional attitudes," because they consist in a relationship between an agent and a proposition. If I believe that Obama is president, I have an attitude to a proposition.

---

3. Franz Brentano. *Psychology from an Empirical Standpoint,* ed. Linda L. McAlister (Milton Park, Abingdon, Oxon.: Routledge, 1995), p. 152.

I used to think the terminology of "propositional attitudes" was a harmless mistake, but in fact it is almost invariably disastrous. It gives *exactly the wrong account* of intentionality. There is indeed a relation if I believe that Obama is president, but the relationship is between me and Obama himself, not between me and a proposition. I do not have any attitude toward the proposition. Some beliefs are attitudes towards propositions. If I believe that Bernoulli's principle is boring, then I do have an attitude toward a proposition—namely, the proposition that states Bernoulli's principle—I think it is boring. But this is a very unusual belief. Most beliefs are not about propositions. They are about people, objects, states of affairs, etc. In the belief we are considering, the proposition is not the *object* of the belief, it is the *content* of the belief. Indeed, thought of in the right way, it is the belief itself. The belief that Obama is president of the United States just consists in that proposition as believed. There is not some further relationship between the agent and some representation. In this case the belief just is the believed representation.

4. PROPOSITIONS AS ABSTRACT ENTITIES

Another related muddle derives from the fact that there is a sense in which propositions are "abstract entities." Suppose that I see that it is raining and I believe that it is raining; then in some crucial respects, my visual experience and my belief have the same propositional content. But it is a muddle to suppose that somehow an abstract entity, the proposition, would have to be seen (in the case of the visual experience) or part of the thought (in the case of the conscious belief that it is raining). This is such a hopeless confusion and I am embarrassed to have to correct it. But here is the correction. Talk of an abstract entity is a manner of speaking by which we describe that which is in common to the visual experience and the thought. It is the delineation of a certain set of conditions of satisfaction. But both visual experiences and thoughts are realized in concrete biological phenomena in the brain. If they were not concrete entities, they could not function causally in our behavior. To talk of propositions is a way of abstracting a common feature in different biological phenomena. If I go for a walk in the Berkeley Hills and you go for the same walk in the Berkeley Hills, then we can talk about a commonality, "the same walk." But it does not follow that walking is having a relation to an abstract entity. This is just a manner of speaking that enables one to speak about something in common. But similarly with intentional states: we need to talk about a common content to different sorts of states. In the example we are considering, I both see that it is raining and think that it is raining. But this does not turn visual experiences and conscious thoughts into abstract entities, nor are they relations to abstract entities. The fact that one can abstract a common propositional content and discuss it in a way that is independent of its realization does not show that it lacks a concrete realization.

If you make these mistakes, they determine a certain conception of intentionality. Intentionality consists invariably of some sort of representation, and the person who has the intentional state has some sort of relation to these representations. For example, John Campbell, who rejects an intentionalistic theory of perception, rejects it on the ground that on such a conception having a perception would be like reading a newspaper about the real world.[4] If you think that all intentionality is a matter of relation to a representation, that the object of the intentionality is the representation, then on an intentionalistic account of perception the awareness in the hallucination must have the same kind of object as the awareness in a veridical perception. In both cases one is aware only of representations. On this view it will seem to you that an intentionalistic account of perception involves a

4. Campbell, John. *Reference and Consciousness.* Oxford: Oxford University Press, 2002. p. 122.

denial of Naïve or Direct Realism. This conception of intentionality is totally mistaken. And one of the main aims of this book is to present an account of perception that definitely refutes it as far as perceptual experiences are concerned. Perceptual experiences are direct presentations of their conditions of satisfaction, and they are experienced as caused by their conditions of satisfaction.

5. THE AMBIGUITY IN "CONDITION"

The notion of a *condition* and *conditions of satisfaction* is systematically ambiguous between the requirement and the thing required. If I believe it is raining, then the requirement in order for the belief to be true is that it be raining. But the fact in the world that satisfies that requirement is the condition in the world, *the fact that it is raining.* This is a common ambiguity in language, commonly called in grammar books, the "process-product" ambiguity. "Condition" (especially "truth condition"), "criterion," and "test" all have the same ambiguity. And the context is usually sufficient to disambiguate the ambiguity. But where the context is inadequate, I will explain in which sense the expression "conditions of satisfaction" is used.

6. REPRESENTATION AND PRESENTATION

Though all intentional states with propositional content and direction of fit are representations of their condition of satisfaction, some of those representations are presentations. When I think about something, my thoughts are representations of whatever it is that I am thinking about. But when I directly perceive it—when, for example, I see it—then my visual experiences are actual presentations of the object and state of affairs seen. More about this in the next chapter.

7. OBSERVER INDEPENDENT AND OBSERVER RELATIVE INTENTIONALITY

Human and animal mental states have an intentionality that is independent of any outside observer's attitude. If I believe that it is raining, then I have that belief regardless of what anybody else thinks. It is intrinsic to that very mental state that it is that very belief, in the sense that it could not be that mental state if it was not that belief. But humans also have the capacity to impose intentionality on sentences, pictures, diagrams, and other sorts of representations. These also have intentionality, but their intentionality is derived, or observer relative. The sentence, "It is raining" has intentionality only relative to speakers of English. However, my belief that it is raining has an intrinsic, or observer independent, intentionality.

Whenever there is an observer relative phenomenon—such as language, property, money, government, and universities—there is an element of ontological subjectivity in its mode of existence. Something is a sentence of English or a piece of American money only because people have certain attitudes toward it. Those attitudes are ontologically subjective. The crucial point for the present discussion is that the ontological subjectivity of a domain does not prevent us from having an epistemically objective set of statements about that domain. The fact that "It is raining" is a sentence of English is ontologically subjective. But of course epistemically it is a completely objective fact that it is a sentence of English.

8. INTENTIONALITY IS PART OF OUR BIOLOGY

A common mistake is to suppose that there is something mysterious about intentionality and that we must explain its possibility by reducing it to something else. But intentionality is a biological phenomenon. If you think that it must be extremely mysterious, then think about simple biological forms of intentionality such as feeling hungry or thirsty. The fact that an animal feels hungry (an intentional state) is no more mysterious than the fact that the animal intentionally eats (an intentional action), and neither of these is more mysterious than the fact that the animal digests what it has eaten. We are talking at every level about biology. There is nothing intrinsically mysterious about intentionality.

9. INTENTIONAL CAUSATION

The cases of intentional causation occur when the intentional content of an intentional state functions as either cause or effect in a causal relation. In the case of bodily intentional acts, the intentional content functions as a cause of the bodily movement. In the case of perception, the state of affairs perceived functions as the cause of the perceptual experience of it. It is going to turn out, in Chapters 4 and 5, that presentational intentional causation is the key to understanding the content of perceptual intentionality.

There is a woefully inadequate conception of causation widespread in philosophy, and as far as I can tell it is due to Hume. The idea is that causation is always a relation between discrete events ordered in time and always instantiates a universal law. I believe, on the contrary, that causation is pretty much everywhere and it is constant. The four basic forces are the weak and strong nuclear forces, gravity, and electromagnetism. None of these is a discrete event; they are pervasive and ubiquitous. Most of the cause-and-effect relations one deals with in everyday life do not instantiate laws. Think, for example, of the causes of the current recession, or the causes of the Republican defeat in the 2012 elections, or the causes of the success of Apple Computer. All of these have components that are describable in the vocabulary of laws, such as the law of gravity, but there are no laws that fit the cause-and-effect relations using the terminology of the laws. This is not a book about causation, I just want to call attention to the fact that in our experience the primary experience of causation is where our own conscious mental states function as either a cause or an effect and do so in virtue of their intentional content. More about this in the rest of the book.

10. NETWORK AND BACKGROUND

Another common mistake is to suppose that intentional states function atomistically—one state at a time. But in general, for humans, intentional states only come as part of a Network of other intentional states. I, for example, cannot believe that Barack Obama is president without believing a whole lot of other things. I cannot want to go skiing without wanting and believing a whole lot of other things. In addition, I have to presuppose a Background of abilities that enable these intentional states to determine their conditions of satisfaction. Theorists will want a general statement, and here it is. In general, intentional states only determine their conditions of satisfaction within a Network of intentional states against a Background of pre-intentional capacities. I have never been able to make a principled distinction between the Network and the Background, and I now think it is theoretically impossible to do so. But the intuitive idea of each is clear enough.

The quickest way I can summarize many of the basic relations in intentionality is with the accompanying chart. If you understand the details of the chart, you will understand intentionality better than many professional philosophers. (The downward arrow ↓ means mind-to-world; the upward arrow ↑ means world-to-mind.)

	Cognition			Volition		
	Perception	Memory	Belief	Intention-in-action	Prior intention	Desire
Direction of fit	↓	↓	↓	↑	↑	↑
Direction of causation	↑	↑	N/A*	↓	↓	N/A
Causally self-reflexive?	yes	yes	no	yes	Yes	no
Presentation or Representation	Pres.	Rep.	Rep.	Pres.	Rep.	Rep.

* N/A means not applicable

Consciousness

Any account of perception must contain an account of conscious perception. But any account of conscious perception must contain, or at least presuppose, an account of consciousness in general. This brief appendix will contain an account of human and animal consciousness. It is important to do this because more false—even unintelligent—things are said about consciousness than just about any other subject in philosophy. It is important to avoid the mistakes before we even get started on a thorough account of perception. The account will be brief because it is a summary of what I have argued for elsewhere.[1] Readers familiar with the history of philosophy will recognize this as containing a "solution" to the so-called "mind-body problem." Here goes.

1. THE DEFINITION OF CONSCIOUSNESS

Consciousness is sometimes said to be hard to define. But if we are just talking about a common-sense definition that identifies the target of analysis, then the definition is rather easy. Consciousness consists of all our states (processes, events, etc.) of feeling or sentience or awareness. These typically begin when we wake up from a dreamless

1. Searle, John R. *The Rediscovery of the Mind.* Cambridge, MA: MIT Press, 1992.
   Searle, John R. *The Mystery of Consciousness.* New York: The New York Review of Books, 1997.

sleep or some other form of unconsciousness and continue until we become "unconscious" again. Dreams are a form of consciousness, though quite different from waking consciousness. The absolutely essential feature of consciousness is that for any conscious state, there is something that it feels like to be in that state. The essence of consciousness is that it is *qualitative* in the sense that there is some experiential quality to any conscious state. It is ontologically *subjective* in the sense that it exists only as experienced by a human or animal subject. And it is *unified* in the sense that all of our conscious states come to us as part of a unified conscious field. I used to think that qualitativeness, subjectivity, and unity were separate phenomena, but I now think each implies the next and, taken together, they constitute the essence of consciousness. The qualitative character of experience implies ontological subjectivity, and those two together imply unity because if you try to imagine your present conscious field broken into seventeen parts, you would not have one conscious field in seventeen pieces but seventeen separate conscious fields.

2. FEATURES OF CONSCIOUSNESS

Consciousness so-defined has many features, but for our purposes the following are the most important. I emphasize them because they are frequently denied in the philosophical literature.

1. Consciousness is real and irreducible. You cannot show that it is an illusion in a way that sunsets and rainbows are illusions, because if you consciously have the illusion that you are conscious, then you are conscious. The illusion/reality distinction presupposes the distinction between how things consciously seem to you and how they really are. But where the existence

of consciousness is concerned, you cannot make that distinction because your conscious illusion of consciousness is the reality of consciousness.

Because consciousness has a subjective or first-person ontology it cannot be reduced to anything that has a third-person or objective ontology.

2. All conscious states so-defined are caused by neuronal processes in the brain. We do not know the details, but given our present understanding of neurobiology there is no doubt that consciousness is caused by neurobiological processes. Though consciousness is *ontologically irreducible*, it is *causally reducible* to brain processes. What does that mean? It means that all of the features of consciousness, without exception, are caused by neurobiological processes in the brain.

3. All of our conscious states are realized in the brain, again, without exception. All known states of consciousness exist in human and animal brains. Perhaps one day we will be able to invent conscious machines out of inorganic materials, but at present the only known consciousness is in human and animal nervous systems.

4. Consciousness with all of its touchy-feely, "mysterious," ontologically subjective features is a biological, and therefore physical, part of the real world. As such, it enters into causal relations with other parts of the physical world. Thus, for example, all of my conscious perceptions are caused in my brain by the impact of perceptual stimuli on my nervous system. And these perceptions in turn together with other processes, some conscious some unconscious, cause my physical behavior. For example, I see the glass of beer in front of me, so I reach out with my hand, take it, and drink from it. Some

people still think that the ontological irreducibility of consciousness makes consciousness not a part of the physical world. They are mistaken. My reaching for the beer is a conscious intentional action on my part, and my movements are caused by my conscious intentions. But anything at all that causes that movement must cause the secretion of acetylcholine, the neurotransmitter specific to bodily movements. So the very conscious state which is qualitative, subjective, touchy-feely, etc. must have a lower-level description in which it is a biological process causing the secretion of acetylcholine. This is no more mysterious than the fact that my car engine has a higher-level description where the explosions in the cylinder move the piston, and a lower-level description where the oxidation of hydrocarbon molecules releases heat energy.

5. All conscious perceptual experience occurs as part of a total conscious field. It is important to remind ourselves of this because some authors who write about perception treat it as existing in isolation. It does not. I cannot consciously see the glass of beer in front of me without having a whole lot of other conscious states as part of my total subjective conscious field.

3. SOME MISTAKEN ACCOUNTS OF CONSCIOUSNESS IN PERCEPTION

In theories of perception, there are two alternatives to the view I have just presented. One is that perceptual consciousness does not exist at all. This view is so implausible it is hard to imagine anyone ever defending it. People who deny that consciousness exists do not do so by saying bluntly, "Consciousness does not exist," nor even, "Perceptual consciousness does not exist." But what they say is consciousness is really something else. In Daniel Dennett's case, he says it is really just a computer program running in the brain. And in John Campbell's case, he says conscious perception is just a direct relation between the perceiver and the object perceived. The only elements in the perceptual situation, according to Campbell, are the perceiver, the object perceived and the point of view.[2] I discuss his views in more detail in Chapter 6.

A second view that I think equally implausible is that perceptual consciousness can exist outside the brain. One example is in the article by Alva Noë, "Experience Without the Head."[3] Noë gives several examples and arguments to attempt to show that the *content*, i.e., the intentional content of our perceptual experiences, is very often determined by very complex relations between ourselves, our dispositions and the environment. He concludes with the following thought (p. 429), "Upshot: it is an open empirical possibility that our experience depends not only on what is represented in our brains, but on dynamic interactions between brain, body and environment. The substrate of experience may include the non-brain body and the world." The problem with this is that the first sentence does not imply the second sentence. It is indeed the case that our experience depends not only on what is represented in our brains, "but on dynamic interactions between brain, body and environment." I take that as an obvious point. But the fact that the content of our experiences depend on these "dynamic interactions" in no way implies anything about the *substrate* of experience. If the substrate of experience means what it is supposed to mean—namely, how the experience is realized—there is no way that qualitative conscious subjectivity could be realized, for example, in the table that I now see or the air that surrounds the table.

2. Campbell, John. *Reference and Consciousness.*
3. Noë, Alva. "Experience Without the Head." *Perceptual Experience.* J. Hawthorne and T. Gendler, eds. Oxford: Oxford University Press, 2006: 411–33.

Remember, when you talk about conscious states, you are talking about actual empirical physical events that have spatial locations, temporal beginnings and ends, spatial dimensions as well as electrochemical properties of various kinds. There just is not any question about that. And these are indeed the result of "dynamic interaction," though of course that is not in conflict with the idea that the dynamic interactions are "represented in the brain." The mistake is to think that this would go any way towards showing that qualitative subjectivity, so to speak, floats around. It does not. It is located in human and animal brains. The first sentence contains an implicit opposition which is false. What is represented in our brains can well be dynamic interactions between brain, body, and environment. Specifically the dynamic interactions between the body and the environment produce effects on our nervous systems. Different neuronal structures in different neuronal architectures fire at different rates, for example. Such processes are sufficient to produce all forms of consciousness. What is the problem supposed to be?

The decisive argument against consciousness existing outside the brain is that like any other higher-level biological feature of the world, such as digestion, photosynthesis, or lactation, consciousness has to be in some biological system. It has to be realized, for example, in some system composed of cells. Perhaps we can create consciousness in non-organic systems, but the biological principle is an instance of a much more general principle which states that any higher-level features at all—such as the liquidity of water, the solidity of the table, and the elasticity of the steel bar—have to be realized in lower-level elements. If we think of consciousness as existing outside human and animal nervous systems as, so to speak, floating around in the air or in the structure of the table, then we have to suppose that the air molecules and the table molecules are realizing consciousness. The idea is not worth serious consideration.

Chapter 2

The Intentionality
of Perceptual Experiences

I have now said something about the history of one of the greatest mistakes in Western philosophy over the past several centuries. As I have described it, the mistake derives, at bottom, from a failure to understand the intentionality of perceptual experience. How exactly? There are two phenomena in the conscious perceptual situation: there are ontologically subjective, conscious perceptual experiences in the head, and the ontologically objective states of affairs and objects in the world perceived, typically outside the head. If you fail to understand that the experience is a direct intentional presentation of the state of affairs, you are likely to think there is only one thing present in the perceptual situation, either the state of affairs perceived or the perceptual experience itself. After all, there is only one experience! The Great Philosophers from Descartes to Kant thought the object of perception is the subjective experience itself. Many philosophers who accept that there is an independently existing object think that if there are two things in the perceptual situation—the experience and the object—then each must be perceived.

Among adherents of a recent theory called Disjunctivism, some have thought that there is no subjective experiential content common to both the veridical and hallucinatory cases. Disjunctivism is a very strange view, and I will tell you more about it in Chapter 6.

Right now, I am going to offer an intentionalistic theory of perception. I think if we are clear about the intentionality of perceptual experiences, most of the philosophical problems have rather obvious solutions. The views I am militating against include both the false view that the subjective experience itself is the object of perception (the Bad Argument) and the equally false view that there is no subjective perceptual experience at all common to both the hallucinatory and veridical cases (Disjunctivism).

The philosophical tradition suffers from presenting overly simple examples of visual perceptions. Philosophers typically talk about such things as seeing tomatoes (H. H. Price)[1] or seeing a piece of wax (Descartes).[2] Let us describe a more realistic scene: I am now looking at San Francisco Bay out of the upstairs study of my house in Berkeley. I see the city of Berkeley in the foreground, the Bay in the background, and on the distant horizon the city of San Francisco, the Golden Gate Bridge, and the hills of the Peninsula. In the immediate foreground, I also see the table on which I am working, the computer with its illuminated screen, various books and papers on the table, and my dog, Tarski, sitting on the floor at my feet. This is a continuous visual experience and I can shift my attention at will. I can even shift my attention without shifting my eyes. I can focus my attention on different aspects of the scene. Sometimes, for the sake of simplicity, in this discussion I will concentrate on certain elements, for example, seeing the table, but we should keep the complexity of this scene in mind as we proceed.

---

1. Price, H. H. *Perception*. London: Metheuen & Co. Ltd, 1973, Chapter 2.
2. Descartes, René. "Meditations on First Philosophy." *The Philosophical Writings of Descartes, Volume II*, trans. J. Cottingham, R. Stoothoff, D. Murdoch. Cambridge: Cambridge University Press, 1984, Meditation II.

I. SKEPTICISM ABOUT THE INTENTIONALITY OF PERCEPTION

Some authors have even doubted the existence of perceptual experiences as qualitative, ontologically subjective experiences produced in the visual system. Let me start by establishing their existence. As you are looking at the scene of San Francisco Bay, close your eyes: Something stops, but the objective visual scene did not stop. It goes on as before. What stopped was your seeing that scene. Yes, and what stopped when you stopped seeing that scene? Well, a number of things. But most prominently you stopped having the visual experiences, and the reason you stopped having them was that the scene stopped producing the stimulations of your retina that eventually (after about 500 milliseconds) resulted in the visual experiences. To repeat the point made earlier, the visual scene includes both the ontologically objective state of affairs perceived and the ontologically subjective experience going on inside your head. I cannot imagine how any sane philosopher can deny the existence of either of these, but I have to tell you that, in one way or another, they have been denied.

Some authors have argued that visual experiences lack intentionality. This view I find frankly flabbergasting because perceptual experience (along with intentional action, and such biologically primitive forms as hunger and thirst) is the paradigm of intentionality, and other forms of intentionality—such as beliefs—are in large part derived from the intentionality of perceptual experiences. For example, I come to *believe* that there are ships in San Francisco Bay on the basis of *seeing* that there are such ships. The biologically primary intentionality of the visual experience is the basis on which I form the belief with that intentional content.[3]

---

3. It is an odd historical fact that analytic philosophers were reluctant to recognize the intentionality of perceptual experiences. I find nothing, for example, in Quine and Davidson, not to

Given that the claim is controversial, we are not justified in simply assuming that perceptual experiences have intentionality. Let us now justify the claim. The first step would be to ask the skeptic for a definition of intentionality. And on the standard definition, intentional states are those that are *of*, or *about*, or *directed at* objects and states of affairs in the world, typically independent of the intentional state itself. Visual and other perceptual experiences obviously meet that definition. As I look at the scene I was describing earlier, my experiences are literally—there is no metaphor involved here—*of* the objects and states of affairs I see, the trees and the Bay as well as the desk, the computer, the books, etc. In an ordinary understanding of the metaphor of direction, they are directed at objects and states of affairs. It is less natural to say that they are *about* objects and states of affairs, and that is because they are presentations rather than representations, an important point that I will get to in a moment. So visual experience meets the standard definition of intentionality.

However, the skeptic might still object that the argument is based on a grammatical illusion. The grammar of sentences of the form "I believe that p" looks a lot like "I see that p," and this creates the illusion that vision is intentional. But if we were to take this skepticism seriously, we would go through the steps and show that the features that are defining of intentionality are characteristic of visual experiences.

mention Carnap or Reichenbach, to suggest that they recognize the intentionality of visual experiences. Quine and Davidson thought of perception as essentially a causal process which causes us to have beliefs. But the idea that there might actually be a logical relation between, for example, the intentional content of my seeing that is raining and my believing that it is raining is totally foreign to their whole way of thinking. Of course, they are right in thinking that there is a causal relation, but the form of causation in question is precisely intentional causation. In the classical period of analytic philosophy, it was typically thought that intentionality must somehow be essentially tied to language, and many thought, as Davidson said explicitly, that an animal could not have beliefs if it did not have a language. This is worse than bad philosophy, it is bad biology: but the first step in overcoming it is to see that the animal relates to the environment by way primarily of the presentational intentionality of its perceptual experiences (and intentional actions).

Just as when I have a belief, it seems to me that the belief represents how things are in the world, when I have a visual experience, it seems to me that the world is the way that I am perceiving it as being. Of course, just as I might discover that my belief is false, so I might discover that my visual experience is not veridical. In that case I have a visual experience that is not satisfied in exactly the same sense in which my beliefs are not satisfied when they are not true, and in which my desires are not satisfied when they are not fulfilled, and so on through other standard forms of intentionality. In short, visual experiences have four features sufficient for intentionality:

1. *Intentional Content.* The actual experiential character of perceptual experience has all the earmarks of intentionality. There is no way I can look out the window without it at least visually seeming to me that San Francisco Bay is in front of me, along with all the other things that I mentioned. Now, that *seeming* is a mark of intentionality. In visual experiences there is a *content*. There is no way you can have this very experience, even if you think it is a hallucination, without it at least seeming to you that you are seeing San Francisco Bay. So this is the first point: the sheer phenomenology, the sheer experiential character of your perceptual experiences, gives you an impression that *this is how things are.* And that is a sure mark of intentionality. I will summarize this point using the usual lame metaphor of "content" by saying perceptual experiences have *intentional content.*

2. *Direction of Fit.* Intentional states have different ways of relating to their conditions of satisfaction. Beliefs are supposed to represent how things are in the world; the belief is supposed to fit the world. Desires and intentions are not supposed to fit pre-existing reality, but rather, if satisfied, reality matches or comes to match the desire or the intention. Of the first category, beliefs, we can say they have the mind-to-world direction of fit. Of the second category, desires and intentions, they have the world-to-mind direction of fit. For beliefs, the belief is in the mind. If it succeeds, it is supposed to

match the world. For desires, if the desire in the mind succeeds, the world is supposed to match the content of the desire. Given this distinction in different directions of fit, perceptual experiences obviously have a direction of fit. Like belief, the direction of my perceptual experience is mind-to-world. Unlike my desires and intentions, my perceptions are not aimed at changing the world to match the content of my experiences, rather the experiences come to me as presenting how the world is. So perceptual experience has both content and direction of fit.

Unlike beliefs and statements, we do not say that our visual experiences are true or false, but this is because they are presentations and not just representations. Truth and falsity are used for propositional representations, such as beliefs and statements, but we need a word to describe success and failure for perception, and, as I remarked earlier, philosophers use the somewhat ugly expression "veridical" to mean the feature of perception that corresponds to truth in beliefs and statements.

3. *Conditions of Satisfaction.* It ought to be obvious from everything I have said that perceptual experiences like beliefs, intentions, and desires will be either satisfied or not satisfied. The world will either be or not be the way it perceptually seems to me. And again to repeat a point made earlier, even in cases where I know the perceptual experience is illusory—as for example, in the famous Müller-Lyer illusion (Fig. 2.1)—all the same, it does seem that the two lines are of different lengths. And that means that the conditions of satisfaction are that they are of different lengths, even though I know as a matter of fact, independently, that those conditions of satisfaction are not in fact satisfied.

So we have three features of perceptual experiences that together are sufficient for intentionality: content, direction of fit, and conditions of satisfaction. The content determines what features of the world are presented by the perceptual experience, the direction of fit is obviously mind-to-world, and the conditions of satisfaction are fixed by the content.

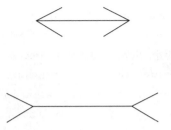

Figure 2.1

4. *Causal Self-reflexivity*. Perceptual intentionality, like memory and prior intentions, but unlike beliefs and desires, has as part of its conditions of satisfaction a causal relation between the intentional state and the external world. And we can put that in one sentence simply by saying the intentional state is not satisfied—we are not perceiving the world in such a way that the intentional content would be satisfied—unless the world's being that way causes us to perceive it that way. This causally self-reflexive feature is a crucial feature of the intentional content of the perceptual experiences. As I said, it is also shared by memory, prior intentions, and intention-in-action, but it is not a universal feature of intentionality. If I believe that Sally is a Republican, then my belief can be true even if Sally's being a Republican does not cause that belief. If I desire to marry a Republican and I marry a Republican, then my desire is satisfied even if the desire did not cause the marriage. But if I see the green table in front of me, then I really see that table only if the presence and features of the table cause the visual experience that I describe when I say, "I see the table." There is a causally self-reflexive feature in the intentional content of perceptual experiences.

To summarize, the visual experience not only meets the definition, but has all the formal features of intentionality. It has a content that determines the conditions of satisfaction, it has a direction of fit, and the content has to set conditions such that the visual experience is either satisfied or not, it either succeeds or fails, in exactly the same way that beliefs and desires, as well as intentions and memories, do. It has an additional feature shared by some, but not all, forms of intentionality: Their conditions of satisfaction are causally self-reflexive. It is part of the conditions of satisfaction that unless the object or state of affairs apparently perceived causes the experience of perceiving it, the experience is not satisfied.

The deepest argument for the intentionality of visual perceptual experiences is one that I have not yet stated, and is one that in the present philosophical era, it is difficult for many philosophers to understand. The proof of this is that they mistakenly suppose that it is an argument *against* the intentionality of perception when in fact it is the most powerful argument *in favor*. It is called the *Argument from Transparency*, and here is how it goes. If you try to describe the subjective visual experience in your head, what you will find is that you are giving the same description that you would give of the state of affairs in the world. The subjective experience is described by saying "I seem to see San Francisco Bay, etc." In order to get rid of the ambiguity in the scope of "seem" I could put this even more precisely by saying "I am having a visual experience which is exactly as if I were seeing San Francisco Bay, etc." The objective state of affairs in the world is described by saying "I see San Francisco Bay, etc." Now, that fact requires explanation. Remember, we have an ontologically subjective visual experience existing entirely as a "private" entity in the head of the perceiving agent, and we have an ontologically objective "public" entity in the world outside the head. How can the description be the same? I think the answer is obvious, and the aim of this chapter is to spell it out. But in short form, it is that the conscious experience is itself a presentation of the state of affairs that constitutes its conditions of satisfaction. So the description of the content of the presentation has to match the state of affairs that constitutes its conditions of satisfaction in the external world. The transparency of the relation between the subjective content in the head and the objective state of affairs in the world is an important phenomenon. I will have a lot to say about it both in this chapter and later.

II. SPECIAL FEATURES OF PERCEPTUAL INTENTIONALITY

So far, visual experiences would sound rather boring, not much more interesting than beliefs or desires. I think their spectacular character derives from their special differences from other forms of intentionality. They are, as I said earlier, along with intentions-in-action, hunger, thirst, and raw emotions, the most basic forms of intentionality. Most of their special features derive from the fact that they are presentational, not just representational. I now want to describe these special features.

1. *Consciousness.* The specific form of presentational intentionality exemplified by my case of looking out my window at San Francisco Bay requires that the perception be conscious. There is so much discussion of unconscious perception in such forms as blind sight and subliminal perception that philosophers have neglected the fact that the full non-pathological forms of perceptions are fully conscious. Try to imagine what it would be like to see the scene I am describing while being totally unconscious of it. It is very hard to understand how you would be able to distinguish perception from just registering, just being able to respond differentially to features of the environment. But the full glory of human visual experience, when the agent is not blind or otherwise impaired, requires full consciousness of the visual scene. This is a consequence of the fact that the visual experience is a presentation and not merely a representation. I am presented with an entire scene, from the Golden Gate Bridge in the distance to the table, and my dog, Tarski, in my immediate foreground,

and everything in between. Beliefs can be either conscious or unconscious, and in fact most of our beliefs are unconscious most of the time. But you cannot have this visual experience, the one I am having right now, without its being conscious.

2. *Presentation Not Representation.* The essential feature of visual experience in which it differs from, for example, belief, even conscious belief, is that it is *presentational* and not representational. The visual experience is not an independent entity that represents the objects and state of affairs I am seeing; it gives me *direct perception* of those objects and states of affairs. My beliefs, for example, are a series of propositional *representations*. But that is not how it is with visual experience. In the present scene, where I am looking at San Francisco Bay, I have a conscious direct perception of the entire scene. Technically speaking, if we define "representation" as anything that has conditions of satisfactions, then presentations are species of representations. All the same, we need to contrast presentations with representations generally, and you will not understand the special intentionality of perception unless you see its presentational character.

3. *Direct Causation.* The presentational intentionality of the perceptual experience derives from the fact that it is experienced as directly caused by the conditions of satisfaction. When you see the object, you experience the object as causing your experience of it. This is even more obvious in the case of touch: when you run your hand along the top of the table, you experience the sensation in your hand as caused by the pressure on the surface of the table.

Some philosophers have difficulty seeing the causal component of visual experience, so let me give an argument that shows it conclusively. Imagine that you have the capacity to form visual images in your imagination that were just as vivid as actually seeing an object. Close your eyes and form a mental image of the scene around you and imagine that you had the capacity to form a mental image that had as much "force and vivacity" (to use Hume's expression) as actually seeing the scene. All the same, there would be a tremendous difference in the phenomenology, because in the case of seeing the scene, you experience the visual experience involuntarily. If you have your eyes open, you are forced to experience the visual experience by the presence of the scene in front of you. You experience the experiences as caused by the scene you are seeing, whereas the visual images that you voluntarily form are experienced as caused by you. The causal component is crucial to all perceptual experience. You have your perceptual experiences as caused by the objects in the world, and you experience them phenomenologically as caused by the objects in the world. This is not in general true with representations. One may have an obsessive memory or obsessive forms of behavior. But there is a special quality to the causal component of perception, and indeed it is the source of presentational intentionality: you experience the object as causing your perception of it. And of course the same point holds with actions, with the opposite direction of fit and direction of causation. When you raise your arm intentionally, you experience the arm going up as caused by the intention-in-action. The causation is part of the content of the experience itself. In the same way in perception, the causation is part of the content of the experience itself.

It is important to emphasize that the five traditional modes of perception—hearing, taste, smell, touch, and vision—are causal throughout. Our perceptual experiences are everywhere experienced as causal transactions between us and the world. You cannot smell something, taste it, hear it, touch it, or see it without the pervasiveness of the causal relations. In your Background, you have the capacity instantly to distinguish events that are causally dependent on your will and those that are not. Close your eyes and reopen them. Move your head around with eyes open: the movements are entirely up to you, but the causation of brute independently existing reality remains constant. This is totally unlike forming visual images, which—pathologies apart—are entirely dependent on your will. Later on in

Chapters 4 and 5, we will see that this causal component is a central feature of our conception of reality and central also to the explanation of how the sheer raw phenomenology of the subjective visual experiences fixes their intentional content, their conditions of satisfaction.

In normal conscious perceptual experiences, you cannot have the perceptual experience without its seeming to you that what you are perceiving is the cause of your experience. Think of hearing a sudden loud noise or smelling an unpleasant smell or bumping into something in the dark or any number of other cases. In every case, when you have the subjective event in your subjective perceptual field, you experience it as caused by the very thing you are perceiving, even though you cannot identify the thing, even though you do not know what exactly you are hearing, smelling, or bumping into. This is one of the keys, and in a way the main key, to understanding the formation of the intentionality of perceptual experience. More about this in Chapters 4 and 5.

4. Non-detachability. It is a consequence of conscious *presentational* intentionality, of the sort that I have been describing, that in the case where the intentional content is satisfied, where I am actually seeing the scene, that I cannot detach the visual experience and operate on it at will. Contrast visual experience with thoughts, words, or pictures and you will see the difference. I can shift my thoughts at will. I can stop thinking about San Francisco and think about something else or I can examine the thought independently of the thing that it is a thought about. But in the case where I am actually looking at the scene in front of me, there is no way that I can detach these experiences from the actual scene. I cannot shuffle these experiences around at will, the way I can shuffle representations around at will. I can shuffle not only "physical" representations in the form of sentences and maps, but also "mental" representations in the form of beliefs and desires. My beliefs and desires are under my control in the sense that I can think about this belief and this desire whenever I want to; but in this particular case, eyes wide open, the scene in front of me, I cannot shuffle my visual experiences around. They are non-detachable. If you do not understand this point, you will not understand conscious perception, visual or otherwise. This is a point about the phenomenology of experiences. Even if the experience is a hallucination, even if I know that it is a hallucination, it is still *experienced as* directly connected to its conditions of satisfaction.

In his important Nicod Lectures, Tyler Burge[4] compares visual experiences to maps and nouns. The noun stands for the object seen and the map represents the environment seen. I believe these comparisons are mistaken. Nouns can be manipulated freely, as can maps. Both are representations. The visual experience is not in that way a representation. It is experienced as essentially tied to its conditions of satisfaction and not detachable.

The non-detachability of the experience from the object inclines us to say that the object is part of the experience. One can appreciate this urge, but it is a mistake. We still need to distinguish between the conscious experience going on in my head and the object outside my head that the experience is of. There is indeed a sense in which the object is part of the total perception because the visual experience will be satisfied only if there is an object there, and its presence and features cause the visual experience. But the experience itself, the conscious event in my head, has to be distinguished from the object outside my head which the experience is of. The experience presents the object, but the object is neither the ontologically subjective experience nor a part of it. The experience is in my head. The object is in the world outside my head.

To repeat a distinction I made in the last chapter, I will use "experience" to name the mental event in my head that has intentionality

4. Burge, Tyler. Unpublished Nicod Lectures. Paris, 2010.

and "perception" to describe such cases when satisfied. Right now I have the *experience* of seeming to see San Francisco Bay and would be having it even if it were a hallucination, but it is in fact satisfied, so it is a *perception* of San Francisco Bay.

In a way, the most amazing thing about visual experiences is the point that I remarked earlier: the description of the experience and the description of the scene is pretty much the same. The sense in which it is true to say that the object itself is part of the perception of it is simply this: the truth conditions of the sentence "I see San Francisco Bay" require a mention of San Francisco Bay. If there is no Bay there, then I did not actually see it. If I describe what I actually see, I say, "I see San Francisco Bay..." and all the rest of it, that is a description of what is actually in the world that I am seeing. Now then, if I describe the content of my visual experience, what is in my head, I will use exactly the same words in the same order. I will say, "I seem to see San Francisco Bay with the Peninsula on the left and Marin on the right," etc. The descriptions are exactly the same. The description of the content in the head and the description of the objects in the world use exactly the same words in the same order. Why? Well, by now the reader of this book knows the answer to that: because the contents in the head are an intentional presentation of their conditions of satisfaction, and those are the objects in the world that I see. Any theory of perception has to explain this commonality, and only a Direct Realist version of intentionalism of the sort I am advancing can satisfy that condition.

5. *Indexicality*. Because of the conscious presentational non-detachability of the visual experience, it is essentially indexical. It is essentially of the *here* and *now*. I can believe just about anything I want, I can desire anything I want. My desires and my beliefs are not tied to my immediate environment in the way my visual experiences are. But when I open my eyes and look around in broad daylight, it is

not up to me what I see; rather I am, by the very nature of the visual experience, forced to see the here and the now. This has an immensely important logical consequence: All experiences have the same formal intentional content. *This is actually happening here and now* or *this object with these features exists here and now.* Roland Barthes makes an interesting point about photography that we can apply to visual perception.[5] He points out that photographs always have the same intentional content (he uses the Husserlian notion of "Noema," but I gather "Noema" means the same thing as "conditions of satisfaction"). He says all photographs have the Noema, "this event actually happened." I think we can apply that lesson to visual perception because the photograph records what is seen in the visual perception. The content of the visual experience is that this is actually happening right here and now. Notice that this point holds even when I know that the conditions of satisfaction are not satisfied here and now. I look at the star and know it ceased to exist millions of years ago, but all the same I am seeing it as if the shining of the star were happening right here and now. That phrase "seeing it as if" marks intentional content because it fixes the conditions of satisfaction. Because of this presentational indexicality, the visual experience always gives us an entire state of affairs, never just an object by itself, but always that *this object exists here now.* In the lectures I mentioned earlier, Burge tells us there is nothing corresponding to the verb in visual experiences. I believe that is wrong. The visual experience always tells us "this object exists" or "this event is happening right here and now." I think it is misleading to call this a verb because it would assimilate it with representations. The important point I am trying to emphasize is that when

5. Barthes, Roland. *Camera Lucida: Reflections on Photography,* trans. Richard Howard. New York: Farrar, Straus, and Giroux, 1981.

you see something, you get an entire state of affairs, not just an object, and a verbal representation of that state of affairs will require both a noun and a verb, "this object *exists*" or "this event *is happening.*"

6. *Continuousness.* Because the perception presents the environment and because it presents the environment in the here and now, it also presents it in a continuous fashion. Representations such as beliefs have a kind of discreteness. You can break them up into separate units and even manipulate the separate units in a way that you cannot do with visual experiences. Where visual experiences are concerned, you have a continuous presentation of the reality around you, and that continuous presentation is literally called "seeing." The continuousness of the conditions of satisfaction of visual perception is both spatial and temporal. As long as my eyes are open and I am fully conscious and in full light, I continue to see the world around me. The *here and now* of the perception is constantly being transformed into the *then and there.* I can indeed control some of this transformation by shifting my attention. The intentionality of my experience is continuous both spatially and temporally precisely because the world itself is continuous spatially and temporally, and the perception presents the world to me. The non-detachability of the visual experience gives it the same spatial and temporal continuity as the world itself.

The objects and states of affairs that I see in the world have a more or less permanent existence. The subjective visual experiences that present those objects and states of affairs to me are fleeting, temporary processes and events. It can be misleading to speak of the visual experiences as a set of entities, as I have been speaking of them. So it is important to continually remind ourselves we are talking not of permanently existing entities, but continuous processes. What I have been describing in this chapter is the intentional relation between the ontologically subjective processes and the objects and states of affairs that they present.

7. *Determinacy.* Perception gives determinacy in a way that representations do not. Leibniz says that reality is that which is totally determinate. If I have a *belief* that Sally has brown hair, that belief represents the world in an indeterminate way. What exact shade of brown? What exact texture of shade of brown? Sally's actual hair is determinate in all its features, but the representation in the form of a belief is not in that way determinate. But when I am actually *seeing* Sally in front of me in broad daylight at point-blank range, many of those details can be filled in. This is not an incidental feature; it derives from the presentational character of the intentionality. Why? *Because the presentational character of intentionality gives us reality itself; we are not operating with a representation of reality, we are operating with the real world by way of conscious experiences of it.* Conscious perceptual experience is the primary way we get that access to the real world. We perceive objects and states of affairs in the real world in a way that the details are filled in. Verbal descriptions are always indeterminate because the general terms used in the description, such as "Sally has brown hair" or "I saw a red rose," assimilate the determinate to the general category. What we are told is that Sally's hair and the rose are like other brown and red things, but when I am actually seeing a red rose, I do not see what it is *like*, I see *it*.

The visual experience cannot be fully determinate, because it is not reality itself. It is a *presentation* of certain aspects of reality, but not of all. It will be indeterminate in various ways. For example, humans cannot see the infrared and ultraviolet colors of the object that we are perceiving, because of the limitations of our perceptual apparatus. Further limitations on the principle of determinacy are cases where my vision is blurred, where I am unable to focus; I have something wrong with my eyes, etc. But notice that all of these cases are experienced as defective, degenerate, non-veridical, or pathological in various ocular ways. In normal, healthy, perfect vision, reality is presented to you as determinate, though even these cases have the limitation that perceptual intentionality only presents certain aspects.

What I am struggling to express here are the facts both that reality itself is determinate, as Leibniz told us, and the perceptual presentation of reality presents it as determinate. The perceptual experience of the table presents it as determinate in a way that the belief about the table does not present it as determinate, and this is because the visual experience *presents* the table whereas the belief merely *represents* the table. This is a very deep point about vision and touch. They give us direct access to objects and states of affairs. In the non-pathological cases, they give us direct access to the determinate character of reality so that the experiences themselves are in this sense determinate: they present their conditions of satisfactions as totally determinate in a way that is never characteristic of verbal representations. To say, "it is brown" leaves a range. But to see the brown color itself does not in that way leave a range. Even visual images do not have that degree of determinacy.

We can see this better if we contrast sight and touch with hearing, taste, and smell. It is true that in hearing you are directly presented with a physical phenomenon in the world, the sound, but nonetheless the sound is not experienced by you as having the features of a material object. Of course, you know theoretically that the sound is in fact sound waves, but the way it is presented to you is not as wave motions in the air but as a phenomenon that comes without any weight or determinate special dimensions. Similarly, with smells and tastes, you know independently that the smell is constituted by sets of molecules that stimulate nerve endings in your nose, but that is not how you experience it. You experience it as an ontologically objective physical phenomenon, but it lacks the characteristics of material objects. It does not weigh anything, you cannot sit on it, and you cannot hammer a nail into it.

To summarize the characteristics of conscious perceptions that distinguish them from other forms of intentionality are that they are presentational rather than representational, they are experienced as caused by their objects or other conditions of satisfaction, they are experienced as non-detachable, they are indexical, they have continuousness, and they have a determinacy that is not possible for representations, such as sentences. (It is worth pointing out parenthetically that conscious intentions-in-actions have these same features with the opposite direction of fit and direction of causation. When I intentionally raise my arm, my intention in action is presentational, causal, non-detachable, indexical, continuous, and determinate.)

III. VISION AND THE BACKGROUND: YOU HAVE TO LEARN HOW TO SEE

There is a common-sense conception of visual perception that is demonstrably false. It is the conception according to which vision is a matter of the passive reception of stimuli and the production of visual experiences by the neurobiological apparatus. On this conception, two people with normal visual neurobiological equipment confronted with the same stimuli would see pretty much the same thing. We know that this conception is false because of studies done on patients who are born blind or became blind at a very early age and later had their sight restored surgically. They do not have normal vision. On the contrary, it appears that in the early stages of development, the child's visual apparatus, along with the rest of her brain, undergoes enormous changes in response to stimuli and this enables what we think of as normal vision. Edelman is probably right to think of the brain as a selectional mechanism, and in the early years the brain is eliminating neurons at an extremely fast rate.[6] We do not understand the details, but the brain learns how to see normally by reinforcing certain visual pathways and eliminating others. This is a problem for the neurobiologist, but it is of philosophical importance because it is a decisive argument against the idea that as long as the visual system is intact, you will have the same experiences as other people with intact visual systems, given the same or equivalent stimuli.

Just as interesting from our present point of view is the way that cultural, educational, and developmental experiences can affect your visual capacities. An illustration of this is the way in which different people with different cultural Backgrounds respond to the same stimulus such as the same work of art. For example, I believe that once you have looked closely at the works of van Gogh and thought very hard about them, the world never looks quite the same. For instance, in the color plates section following page 74, I present (one version of) his famous painting "The Starry Night" (plate 1). I think if you reflect on this, it will affect your perception of the night sky. The picture is indeed a representation of a starry night, but the conditions of satisfaction of the picture are not that it should be perceptually indistinguishable from the starry night; it is not supposed to be like a photograph. Rather, van Gogh invites us to see the night sky as if it were this way. It is a case of *"seeing-as,"* and I will explain later in this chapter and in Chapter 4 why all seeing has to be *seeing-as*.

Often, visual representations influence our ways of perceiving the reality that they supposedly represent. A famous example, also in the color plates section, is Picasso's portrait of Gertrude Stein (plate 2). When she first saw it, she complained, "But I do not look like that." Picasso said, "You will, Gertrude. You will." I take it part of what is meant by that is that people

6. Edelman, Gerald. *Neural Darwinism: The Theory of Neuronal Group Selection.* New York: Basic Books, 1987.

will then see her as the woman in the picture, and their perception of her will be influenced by the picture.[7]

Illustrations of the way the Background affects our perception are given by examples from Vermeer and Terborch (see plates 3 and 4 in the color plates section). There is a famous Vermeer in the Berlin museums that is subject to different interpretations. When I taught in Berlin, my office was a five-minute walk from the Dahlem Museum, and I had the chance to study this painting very closely over a period of several weeks.[8] The painting shows a man and a woman in rather severe but nonetheless elegant surroundings. The woman is drinking wine from a glass; the man is standing with his hat on, holding a jug of wine in his right hand as he looks at the woman. A standard textbook account of the picture is given in *Vermeer* by Arthur K. Wheelock, Jr. He writes as follows, comparing Vermeer with Pieter de Hooch:

> One major difference exists between *The Glass of Wine* and De Hooch's prototypes: Vermeer's interiors are more elegant. The figures are well dressed, the table is covered with an elaborate rug, the window contains a coat of arms, and the picture on the back wall has a gilded frame. The demeanor of the man and woman is also so proper that no explicit associations of love, such as one might make given the presence of the lute and the glass of wine, can be made.[9]

As I said, I have looked long and hard at this picture, and I think Wheelock's interpretation is mistaken. The picture shows a standard seduction scene. The man, in a word, is trying to get that girl drunk.

7. I do not know if this story about Picasso and Stein is true. It is a historical anecdote commonly repeated. The point, for the present discussion, is that it does not matter if it is historically accurate; the point made by it is philosophically correct.

8. Because of the peculiar history of the location of works of art in Berlin, the paintings have been moved around since the Second World War. What was in the Dahlem museum when I taught in Berlin in 1990 will now be located in one of the other Berlin museums. The last time I saw the picture, it was in the Gemäldegalerie.

9. Wheelock, Arthur K., Jr. *Vermeer and the Art of Painting.* New York: Abrams, 1981, 90.

In one form or another, most of us have been in that scene. How do I know that I am right and Wheelock is wrong? I do not. What I am arguing is that the interpretation of a visual experience, and in particular, the interpretation of a work of art, will be a function of the conceptual apparatus that the interpreter brings to the experience. In my case, I have a totally different reading of the picture from Wheelock's.

Another, even more spectacular, example of different interpretations of the same stimulus is provided by Terborch's famous painting "The Admonition." There are different versions of this picture, and I think I have seen at least two of them. In both cases, Terborch is anxious to show off his fantastic painting ability, painting the folds of the woman's dress. The painting shows a man sitting next to an older woman at a table, confronting a much younger woman with her back turned to us. The standard title of the picture is "The Admonition," or sometimes, "The Paternal Admonition." According to the tradition, the picture shows a man admonishing his daughter for some infraction that is not obvious in the picture. We are to think of the mother as somewhat embarrassed by this as she looks down at her glass of wine. No less a person than Goethe describes the picture as follows:

> As the third they had selected the so-called *Instruction paternelle* of Gerald Terborch, and who does not know Wille's wonderful copperplate of this painting? [*Who indeed?*] A noble knightly father sits with one leg over the other and seems to be admonishing the daughter standing before him. His daughter, a magnificent figure in a white satin dress which hangs in abundant folds, is seen only from behind, but her whole attitude seems to indicate that she is restraining herself. That the admonition is not violent or shaming can be seen from the father's expression and bearing, and as for the mother, she seems to be concealing a slight embarrassment by looking down into a glass of wine which she is in the act of drinking.[10]

10. Goethe, J. W. *Elective Affinities*. New York: Penguin Books, 1971, 191.

I totally disagree with Goethe's interpretation, and I think subsequent commentators are more likely to agree with me. The man in question is not admonishing the girl; he is negotiating with the madam of the establishment the price that he is going to pay for the girl. In at least one earlier version of the painting, the man was actually holding a coin in his hand. A close look at the scene, especially with a big bed in the background, and the spectacular attractiveness of the woman's outfit, the youth of the supposed husband and father, all suggest that it is not a case of a father, mother, and daughter, but of a madam, employee, and a potential client. Once again, there is no way to demonstrate that my interpretation is correct and Goethe's is mistaken, but I think the point that I am making should be obvious. It is not an issue of my arguing with Goethe but of attempting to show how the same visual stimulus will produce totally different reactions in people depending on the Background capacities that they bring to bear on the experience.

All of these reflections lead to a much deeper point which should be made explicit. In The Investigations,[11] Wittgenstein made famous the phenomenon of "seeing-as," as illustrated by the duck-rabbit example that he borrowed from Jastrow.[12] The phenomenon that Wittgenstein described as "seeing-as," the point he was making was that, in this case, you can see the same figure either as a duck or as a rabbit. The philosophical importance of this derives from the fact that the stimulus is held constant. This is a remarkable fact: exactly the same stimulus can produce completely different experiences, even though one is not deceived or otherwise suffering from any of the failures of visual perception—there is no question of hallucination, delusion, illusion, etc. The point I want to emphasize now is that all seeing is "seeing-as," and it must be so because of the intentionality of the visual experience. All visual

---

11. Wittgenstein, Ludwig. *Philosophical Investigations*, trans. by G. E. M. Anscombe. Oxford: Basil Blackwell, 1958, Part II, xi, 194e.

12. Jastrow, J. J. *Fact and Fable in Psychology*. New York: Houghton Mifflin, 1901. Originally from *Harper's Weekly*, November 19, 1892, 1114.

Plate 1. Vincent van Gogh (1853–1890). *The Starry Night* (1889).

Plate 2. Pablo Picasso (1881–1973). *Gertrude Stein.*
1906. Oil on canvas, H. 39-3/8, W. 32 in. (100 x 81.3
cm). Bequest of Gertrude Stein, 1946 (47.106) ©
2014 Estate of Pablo Picasso / Artists Rights Society
(ARS), New York.

Plate 3. Johannes Vermeer (1632–1675). *The Glass of Wine* (ca. 1661).

Plate 4. Gerard ter Borch (1617–1681). *The Gallant Conversation,* known as "The Paternal Admonition" (ca. 1654).

Plate 5. Claude Monet (1840–1926). *Poppies* (1873).

Plate 6. Claude Monet. *Poppies* (1873), with red and green inversion.

Figure 2.2

intentionality is a matter of presentations, presentations are a subspecies of representation, and representation is always under some aspect or other. It is impossible simply to represent or present something *tout court*—one always does it in some aspect or another. Jastrow's illustration, which I have actually seen in the original magazine and is now easily available on the Internet, actually looks like either a duck or a rabbit. But the corresponding crude drawing will exhibit exactly the same ambiguity: either a rabbit looking upward to the left or a duck looking to the right. And this illustrates yet another point about visual experience, the brain has an enormous capacity to take degenerate stimuli and produce from them a visual experience with quite definite conditions of satisfaction. The crude drawing that I made

Figure 2.3

does not look literally like either a duck or a rabbit, yet it is very easy to see it as either.

IV. WHAT HAPPENED TO SENSE DATA?

What then about the existence of sense data? Are there such things? The notion of a sense datum was introduced to provide an object of perceptual awareness. The Bad Argument, in its various forms, seems to have the consequence that one never sees objects and states of affairs in the world, but only one's own subjective experiences. A general term is needed for that and the concept of "sense data" seemed to do the job.

But if the Bad Argument is exposed as fallacious, then what happens to sense data? Do they exist? As usual in philosophy, the answer is that it all depends on what you mean by "sense data." If by "sense data" one means conscious perceptual experiences, then of course sense data exist. But if the question means, are there conscious perceptual experiences that are the objects of perception? Then the answer is no. To say that they are perceived is to state the conclusion of the Bad Argument.

But it is misleading to call them sense data, because, first, they are not the objects of perception; they are the perceivings themselves. And second, they are not, in the ordinary way, data. The idea of a "datum" suggests some sort of evidence. But, for example, if I am looking at a computer in front of me, I do not have evidence that there is a computer there, I literally *see* that there is a computer there.

There is an interesting analogy with the concept of "qualia." Since all conscious experiences are qualitative, there is no point in introducing the notion of qualia. Similarly, with the notion of sense data, since all conscious perceptual experiences are experiences from the senses, it seems redundant to introduce a special notion of sense data.

V. THE BRAIN IN A VAT

A common thought experiment in philosophy is to imagine that all of one's experiences are had by a Brain in a Vat. The thought experiment only makes sense from the first-person point of view, so let us try it from that point of view. I am now seated at my desk on the campus of the University of California. I have a whole sequence of experiences caused by external stimuli, which in turn cause neurobiological processes, which cause my subjective qualitative experiences. The "Brain in a Vat" fantasy asks me to imagine that I am having experiences exactly like these, qualitatively in every respect indistinguishable from these, but in fact I am not sitting in Berkeley. My brain is in a vat of nutrients somewhere in Minnesota in the twenty-fifth century and I am being fed by a very well designed computer program with a set of stimuli such as to render my experiences indistinguishable from the experiences of the person actually living in Berkeley, California, in the twenty-first century. Is it possible to imagine such a thing? I think it clearly is, for a very simple reason: we are in fact brains in vats. The skull is a cranium vat made largely of calcium, but it is roughly spherical and it houses a brain. The difference between it and the fantasy Brain in a Vat is entirely due to the fact that my actual brain vat is situated in my body, and the signals that it receives come into peripheral nerve endings and come through the body. But the point of the thought experiment is simply to imagine that one could have stimuli absolutely indistinguishable from these, and brain processes exactly like these, and qualitative experiences exactly like these, while not being situated in this body located in this environment.

A movie based on a similar premise, *The Matrix*, imagined that groups of people are subject to artificial stimuli that render their experiences indistinguishable from a real life. The fact that millions of people were able to understand the movie is at least evidence that the fantasy is intelligible, that it makes sense even if it is a science-fiction fantasy.

All that is necessary to get the fantasy going are the assumptions that, at any given moment, all of our conscious experiences are caused by processes in the brain. And, in principle, at least one could have those processes minus any connection with the external world of the sort that one is now enjoying. Indeed, strictly speaking, you do not even need these assumptions: all you need is the assumption that for any given conscious experience, it is possible to make a separation between the objective ontology that one is perceiving, or otherwise experiencing, and the subjective ontology of one's conscious experiences. If you grant that it is possible to make that distinction, then it follows that it is possible to imagine a case in which there was a radical dissociation between the objective ontology and the subjective ontology.

I think the Brain-in-a-Vat fantasy is a useful reminder of the ontological difference between the subjective ontology produced in our nervous system and the objective ontology that we have access to through perceptual and other means. However, I seldom appeal to the fantasy because it is so persistently misunderstood. Sometimes people think that if you regard the fantasy as at least intelligible, then you are committed to some skeptical doubts about whether or not we really are brains in vats. I have no such doubts, there is no epistemic point at all in my use of the Brain in a Vat fantasy. I will make use of the Brain in a Vat fantasy in chapters 4 and 5 when we consider how the subjective ontology of our raw experiences fixes certain conditions of satisfaction and not others. The point of the fantasy is to dramatically illustrate the distinction between the subjective ontology of perceptual consciousness entirely in the head and the objective ontology of the real world, which we perceive in perceptual consciousness.

VI. CONCLUSION

I have now achieved the main aims I set for myself in the first two chapters. I exposed the fallacy behind the Bad Argument for the rejection of Direct Realism and the acceptance of the sense datum view. I made a strong claim, not yet fully substantiated, to the effect that this is the greatest disaster in epistemology over the past four centuries. And within this chapter, more importantly, I presented what I think is a correct account of perception that emphasizes the presentational intentionality of the perceptual experience.

There are a number of important questions about the intentionality of perceptual experience that I have not yet discussed but will discuss in later chapters. Specifically, I have not yet discussed how the raw phenomenology of the subjective experiences fixes rich intentional content. This will occupy Chapters 4 and 5. Also, I have been mostly concerned with the perception of things as belonging to a certain type but not of the perception of them as specific tokens. This is a non-trivial issue which in *Intentionality* I call the "Problem of Particularity," and I will discuss this in Chapter 5.

Chapter 3

Further Developments of the Argument Against the Bad Argument

The aim of this chapter is to fill in a large number of the details that have been left out of the account so far. I do not know about God or the Devil, but good philosophy is in the details. In Chapter 1 I made a very strong claim, namely, that historically all of the arguments against Direct Realism, or at least all those known to me, rest on the same fallacy: the fallacy of ambiguity that is manifest in the Bad Argument. I am not going to go through the entire history of the subject, but I will pick out examples from both the classics and more recent texts. You can test for yourself if the arguments that I present against these examples work for other examples. I think they work for all of them. If you are convinced by what I have said that the Bad Argument is pervasive, invalid, and historically of decisive importance, but you find the history of philosophy boring, then you can skip this chapter and go on to the next one.

The Bad Argument survives in an upside-down form in contemporary Disjunctivism. The classical version says that because the good case and the bad case are cognitively the same, they should receive the same analysis. In the bad case we see only sense data, so in the good case we see only sense data. The Disjunctivist accepts the argument as valid but denies the first premise, that the good case and the bad case are cognitively the same. But he thus accepts the worst feature of the Bad Argument, namely that if the good case and the bad case are cognitively similar, then Naïve Realism is false.[1] One of my main claims in this book is that once you see the fallacy in the Bad Argument, you can see both that the experience in both the good case and the bad case have the same cognitive content and that Direct Realism is true. The typical assumption in Disjunctivism is that if there is a common content to the good and bad cases, a "highest common factor" in McDowell's expression,[2] then that common content would be the object of perception and Naïve Realism would be false.

I. CLASSICAL EXAMPLES OF THE BAD ARGUMENT

Not surprisingly, there are different versions of the Bad Argument, but the common feature that runs through them is the confusion between the intentional sense of "aware of," and other such expressions, and the constitutive sense of the same expressions. The essence of the Bad Argument is to treat the experience itself as the object, or possible object, of perceptual awareness in the sense in which real objects in the world when perceived are the objects of perceptual awareness.

I begin with a classic case of Berkeley. He uses the first of the Three Dialogues, between Hylas and Philonus, to establish that all we perceive are our own ideas. To do this, he presents several versions of what I have been calling the Bad Argument. He defines the notion of "sensible things" as "those only which are immediately perceived by sense."[3] And on the

---

1. Formally the shift is from *modus ponens* to *modus tollens*. The original Bad Argument goes: if p (the good and bad cases have the same content), then q (Naïve Realism is false). P, therefore q. The Disjunctivist version goes: if p, then q, but not q (Naïve Realism is true) therefore not p (the good and bad cases do not have the same content). As Gil Harman famously says, "One man's *modus ponens* is another man's *modus tollens*."

2. McDowell, John. "Criteria, Defeasibility, Knowledge," in Alex Byrne and Heather Logue, *Disjunctivism: Contemporary Readings*, Cambridge, MA: MIT Press, 2009, 75–90.

3. Berkeley, George. *Three Dialogues Between Hylas and Philonus*. Indianapolis, IN: Bobbs-Merrill, 1954, 15.

same page, he tells us that sensible things consist of "sensible quali-ties." Sensible things therefore are nothing else but so many sensible qualities or combinations of sensible qualities. By "immediately," he means without any inference. For example, when I see the red table-cloth in front of me, I do not infer that it is red, I see that it is red. In that sense, redness is a sensible quality for Berkeley. I think, by now, the reader will recognize that the notion of "immediate perception" is already subject to the ambiguity that I have been calling attention to, the ambiguity between the "perception" being identical with the object of the perception and the "perception" being an intentional state that has the object of the perception as its intentional object. Here is a famous passage from Berkeley:

PHILONUS: Upon putting your hand near the fire, do you perceive
   one simple uniform sensation or two distinct sensations?
HYLAS: But one simple sensation.
PHILONUS: Is not the heat immediately perceived?
HYLAS: It is.
PHILONUS: And the pain?
HYLAS: True.
PHILONUS: Seeing therefore they are both immediately perceived at the same time, and the fire affects you only with
   one simple or uncompounded idea, it follows that this
   same simple idea is both the intense heat immediately perceived and the pain; and, consequently, that the intense
   heat immediately perceived is nothing distinct from a particular sort of pain.[4]

He concludes that the intense heat is not an ontologically objective phenomenon but exists entirely as an experience in the mind. He extends

4. Berkeley, George. *Three Dialogues Between Hylas and Philonus*, 15.

this argument in different forms to all other "sensible qualities." This argument is a beautiful illustration of the fallacy of ambiguity in the Bad Argument. "Immediately perceived" has two different senses, one where what is immediately perceived is an ontologically objective state of affairs in the world, in this case the heat of an actual fire. This is the intentional sense of "immediately perceived," and in this sense the quality perceived is ontologically objective. In the other sense of "immediately perceived," what is immediately perceived is the sensation itself, the painful sensation of heat. This is the constitutive sense of "immediately perceived," and in this sense the quality perceived is ontologically subjective. Berkeley starts with the first of these in his notion of "immediately perceived," but he then uses the ambiguity to establish that all we perceive are ontologically subjective experiences. I do not believe the fallacy could be more obvious, and in fact the whole of the first dialogue consists in repeated applications of this fallacy.

In Hume, the ambiguity that I have been citing is also manifest. In the very first paragraph of Hume's Treatise he begins the book with the following sentence, "All the perceptions of the human mind resolve themselves into two distinct kinds, which I shall call *impressions* and *ideas*." The notion of perception can mean either the perceptual content of an experience or the thing perceived, and we already know that that is, respectively, the constitutive and the intentional sense of the corresponding verbs. In the sense of perceptual intentional content, I can indeed divide, at least for these purposes, my perceptual experiences into impressions and ideas. Impressions include actual perceptual experiences, such as sensations; and ideas, such things as mental images. But if we are talking about objects perceived, then the "perceptions" of my mind would not include impressions but such things as, for example, trees, mountains, stones and other ontologically objective phenomena. Hume takes it for granted that when I perceive trees and mountains what I am actually perceiving are my own impressions. But that already contains the fallacy that we have been exploring because impressions are always ontologically subjective, and the trees and mountains are ontologically objective. To show the manifestation of the fallacy in Hume, I want to go through the passage I mentioned before and I see no alternative to *explication de texte*.

> 'Twill first be proper to observe a few of those experiments, which convince us, that our perceptions are not possest of any independent existence. When we press one eye with a finger, we immediately perceive all the objects to become double, and one half of them to be remov'd from their common and natural position. But as we do not attribute a continu'd existence to both these perceptions, and as they are both of the same nature, we clearly perceive, that all our perceptions are dependent on our organs, and the disposition of our nerves and animal spirits.[5]

What is meant by "perception" in this passage? I think it is systematically ambiguous. He tells us that it means "all the things we perceive" in the third sentence. But of course, that expression, "all the things we perceive," is itself ambiguous. He means it to include what we normally think of as material objects in the external world, as the subsequent argument shows. He says, "When we press one eye with a finger, we immediately perceive all the objects to become double, and one half of them to be remov'd from their common and natural position." Here, by "objects" he means such things as chairs and tables; and since they are perceptions, he is claiming that when we push one eyeball we perceive them to become double. But, strictly speaking, that is not true. We do not perceive any such thing. It is not "all the objects" that *become* double, rather we *see* them double. That is to say, we have two visual experiences of each object, but we do not, for a moment, see two of anything. It is not the material *objects* in the world that are double, but the visual *experiences*. And this is precisely the ambiguity that we have been pointing to all along. Hume

5. Hume, David. *A Treatise of Human Nature,* ed. L. A. Selby-Bigge. Oxford: Oxford University Press, 1888, 210–11.

goes on, "But as we do not attribute a continu'd existence to both these perceptions, and as they are both of the same nature, we clearly perceive that all our perceptions are dependent on our organs and the disposition of our nerves and animal spirits."

All of our perceptual experiences are indeed dependent on the state of our organs, but it does not follow that objects in the world that we actually perceive are dependent on our organs. So this again is the same ambiguity manifesting itself. The ontologically subjective experiences we have of objects in the external world are dependent on the state of our organs, but the objects in the external world themselves are not, in that way, dependent on the state of our organs. Well, if Hume's description of the case is wrong, then what is the correct description? I believe it is pretty obvious. Here goes: When we press one eye with a finger, we immediately have a visual phenomenon known as "seeing double" or "double vision." I have two visual experiences of each of the objects I am seeing. I do not see the visual experiences, I see the objects; and in this case I see them double. The intentional content is (sort of) as if I were seeing two objects, but in fact I know that I am not seeing two objects. I attribute a continued existence to the object but not to the experiences. If "perception" means perceptual experience, then I would never attribute a continued existence to a perception. Thus, when Hume says, "we do not attribute a continu'd existence to both these perceptions," he is talking about visual experiences and is correct in saying that we could not attribute a continued existence to experiences when they are not being experienced. But if "perception" means the object perceived, then the object perceived remains exactly the same existing independently of my experience of it, whether in double vision or otherwise. So the only passage I know where Hume explicitly uses the Argument from Illusion commits exactly the same fallacy we have discovered in the other authors.

Let us now turn to a more recent author, A. J. Ayer in *The Foundations of Empirical Knowledge*. In developing his argument that all we perceive are sense data, Ayer produces the following passage:

> Nevertheless, even in the case where what we see is not the real quality of a material thing, it is supposed that we are still *seeing something*; and that it is convenient to give this a name. And it is for this purpose that philosophers have recourse to the term "sense-datum". By using it they are able to give what seems to them a satisfactory answer to the question: What is the object of which we are directly aware, in perception, if it is not part of any material thing? Thus, when a man sees a mirage in the desert, he is not thereby perceiving any material thing; for the oasis which he thinks he is perceiving does not exist. At the same time, it is argued, *his experience is not an experience of nothing; it has a definite content.* Accordingly, it is said that he is experiencing sense-data, which are similar in character to what he would be experiencing if he were seeing a real oasis, but are delusive in the sense that the material thing which they appear to present is not actually there.[6]

This paragraph exhibits the fallacy quite starkly. Look closely at the clause, "His experience is not an experience of nothing; it has a definite content." In the intentionalistic sense, his experience is precisely an experience of nothing because in the oasis line of business there is *nothing* there. There is no oasis there, but there is an intentional content in his head. At this point, Ayer has already committed the fallacy of ambiguity when he says, "it (the experience) has a definite content." Precisely, it has an intentional *content* that presents an oasis as the condition of satisfaction, but there is no intentional *object*; hence the content is not satisfied. The fact that the experience has a definite *content*

6. Ayer, A. J.*The Foundations of Empirical Knowledge*. London: Macmillan 1953, p. 4 (emphasis added).

does not show that it has an *object*. The content is not itself the object of the experience, unless, of course, we are using "experience of" in precisely the constitutive and not the intentionalistic sense. When Ayer writes the clauses, "his experience is not an experience of nothing; it has a definite content," he thinks that the second clause substantiates the first, that the existence of the content proves that it is not an experience of nothing. But it does not. The experience is precisely the experience of nothing in the intentionalistic sense. He can only suppose that the existence of the content is a *something* because he is committing the fallacy of ambiguity. The intentional content is only the object in the constitutive, but not in the intentionalistic, sense. If Ayer had written, "it has a definite object," then the falsity would have been apparent. There is no object. But what he has done is treat the expression "experience of" as taking "content" as its direct object. Thus what was originally an experience, which was treated intentionalistically—the agent thinks he is seeing an oasis but he is not seeing *anything*—is now a case where, all the same, the experience is an experience of something because it has a "definite content." I do not believe the fallacy could be more obvious.

Once you are aware of the fallacy, you see it every time you turn around. I opened the pages of Byrne and Logue's book at random and found the following in an article by Howard Robinson, under the heading "The Revised-Successful Causal Argument for Sense Data":

1. It is theoretically possible by activating some brain process which is involved in a particular type of perception to cause an hallucination which exactly resembles that perception in its subjective character.

2. It is necessary to give the same account of both hallucinating and perceptual experience when they have the same neural cause. Thus, it is not, for example, plausible to say that the hallucinatory experience involves a mental image or sense datum, but that the

perception does not, if the two have the same proximate—that is, neural—cause.

These two propositions together entail that perceptual processes in the brain produce *some object of awareness* which cannot be identified with any feature of the external world—that is, they produce a sense-datum.[7]

You could not get a clearer statement of the fallacy than this. The perceptual processes posited in the brain do indeed produce a conscious experience, but that conscious experience is not an object of awareness in the sense in which objects in the external world are objects of awareness. The "object" is identical with the awareness itself. I have been talking as if this ambiguity were like standard ambiguity, such as "bank" in the sentence, "I went to the bank." But of course, one of the legs of the ambiguity is totally bogus. There is no object of awareness except in the trivial Pickwickian sense that you can always use the verb "aware of" to have the expression referring to its own token extension as its direct object. The awareness is of the awareness itself.

II. HOW THE REFUTATION OF THE BAD ARGUMENT AGAINST DIRECT REALISM EXTENDS TO OTHER VERSIONS OF THE ARGUMENT FROM ILLUSION

I said earlier that all the variations of the Argument from Illusion commit the same fallacy of confusing the constitutive sense of "aware of" and other perceptual terms with the intentionalistic sense of

---

7. Robinson, Howard. "Selections from *Perception*," in *Disjunctivism: Contemporary Readings*, 153 (emphasis added).

these expressions. I now want to go through the standard arguments that show how this is the case.

1. The bent stick and the elliptical coin

There are two arguments that are the same in structure, so I will deal with them both simultaneously. If I put a straight stick in water, then it looks bent. This is due to the refractive properties of water whereby the reflection of light waves off the stick is altered by immersion in water. If I hold up a round coin in front of my face and turn it slightly at an angle so I do not see it head on but tilted, it no longer looks round but looks elliptical. So the argument goes: Pedantically, one might object that the stick does not look as a bent stick would look out of water, and the coin would not look as an elliptical coin would look if you saw it head on. But, all the same, let us leave out these pedantic objections and go to the next step. The argument against Direct Realism in these cases claims that I did actually see *something bent* and *something elliptical*; there is no question about that. But the stick is not bent and the coin is not elliptical. We can, if you like, say that I saw the *bent appearance* of the stick and the *elliptical appearance of the coin*, so the elliptical and bent appearances were the objects of my perception. In both cases I did not see the object itself, only appearances. Let us get a name for these; we will call them "sense data." And it turns out, in such cases, I do not see objects but only sense data. And here is the next step: Because the experience is qualitatively indistinguishable in the veridical cases and the illusory cases, I have to give the same analysis to both. And if I do not see the object itself in the illusory cases, then I should say that I do not see the object in the veridical cases.

Superficially the argument from the elliptical coin and the bent stick is different from the hallucination argument. But I think if we go deeply into it, we will find that the argument commits exactly the same fallacy that I have been alleging. So let us spell it out in some detail for the elliptical coin.

I see something elliptical. What is it that I see that is elliptical? Well, literally speaking, it is the appearance of the coin. But now, and this is a crucial step, since what I directly perceive is elliptical and the coin is not elliptical, it seems that I am not directly perceiving the coin. What am I directly perceiving? Well, we already answered that. It is the elliptical appearance. But if I am not seeing the coin (an ontologically objective object), but I am seeing an elliptical appearance, then it appears that the direct object of the verb "see" names some private (ontologically subjective) experience that I am having. There is no elliptical material object present. And then the argument goes through the rest of the steps: Because there is no qualitative difference between seeing the coin veridically and seeing it under its illusory aspect, we should give the same analysis of both. In both cases, we perceive only ontologically subjective phenomena. As with the arguments in Berkeley, Hume, and Ayer, we have shifted from the intentionalistic interpretation of the verbs of perception to the constitutive or identity interpretation of the verbs. A true statement using the verbs requires the presence of a material object or some other ontologically objective phenomenon to meet the conditions of satisfaction provided by the verb. But on the constitutive or identity sense, all that is required is a noun that names an ontologically subjective experience, something that is identical with the perceiving or the awareness.

What is wrong with this argument? There are a number of things wrong with it. But immediately there is one that Austin pointed out,[8] namely, there is no way you can see the appearance of the coin without seeing the coin itself, because the appearance is just the way the coin looks. What is going on? We have already seen that all perception

8. Austin J. L. *Sense and Sensibilia*, ed. G. J. Warnock. Oxford: Oxford University Press, 1962.

is under an aspect, and the same object may present different appearances under different aspects. But in every case, it is the object itself that is seen.

The literally false step in the argument is the one that says: because I directly perceive something elliptical and because the coin itself is not elliptical, it follows that I do not directly perceive the coin. But it does not follow, because the meaning of the sentence, "I see the elliptical appearance of the coin," implies "I see the way the coin looks." And that in turn implies that I see the coin. There is no way I can see the appearance of the coin without seeing the coin. And from the fact that I see that the coin looks elliptical from this point of view and the fact that the coin is not elliptical, it does not follow that I do not see the coin.

The important thing to see in these cases is that the subject does not literally see anything bent or sees anything elliptical. What he sees is something that, under those conditions, "looks bent" or "looks elliptical." But this is not to describe an actual bent or elliptical object of his perception but rather the conditions of satisfaction of a perceptual experience. In both cases, we need to make a distinction between the perceptual experience, which has intentional content which may or may not be satisfied, and the actual object and state of affairs in the world that is perceived, which may be perceived with varying degrees of accuracy.

2. Double vision

We have already discussed Hume's use of the example of "seeing double," but the standard use is slightly different, so I will go through it. Because we have binocular vision, double vision is always possible. You can test this for yourself: hold up your finger in front of your face and focus your eyes on a far wall. A phenomenon will occur known as seeing your finger double. Here is how the Argument from Illusion goes. In the case of seeing your finger double, what did you see two of? You did see two of something, but not two fingers, because there was only one finger there. But all the same, you did *see two of something*. What are those somethings? Get a name for them, call them sense data...and the argument is off and running as it was in the earlier cases. The crucial mistaken step is the one where because we have the phenomenon of seeing the finger double, we think that we should say that we saw two of something. But of course, we did not see two of anything, we saw one finger and we saw it double. Now, how exactly do we analyze that claim? And the answer, I think, is that the experience itself has as its conditions of satisfaction that there should be two fingers there. Of course, we do not for a moment suppose that there are two fingers there, and indeed the quality of these perceptual experiences is really not the same as focusing your eyes on a finger and seeing it in a unitary fashion. What then, exactly, are there two of? The answer is that there are two visual experiences that give two presentations of a finger, but *you do not see the visual experiences*. Rather, the visual experience is the seeing itself and the seeing presents the finger in two forms. In the constitutive sense of "aware of," you are aware of two finger experiences. In the intentionalistic sense, you had the presence of two fingers as conditions of satisfaction, but those conditions were not in fact satisfied because there was only one finger there.

I have been playing along with the standard argument, but I have to issue an objection at this point. The images of the finger in double vision are not really like the image produced when I focus my eyes on the finger and the two images coalesce. The images are, so to speak, transparent in that I continue to see the far wall quite clearly, when I focus my attention to the far wall, even though the finger is in the way.

3. *Macbeth's dagger*

> Is this a dagger which I see before me,
> The handle toward my hand? Come, let me clutch thee.

I have thee not, and yet I see thee still.
Art thou not, fatal vision, sensible
To feeling as to sight? or art thou but
A dagger of the mind, a false creation,
Proceeding from the heat-oppressed brain?
I see thee yet, in form as palpable
As this which now I draw.[9]

Macbeth's dagger is one of the most famous versions of the Argument
from Illusion. It is a variant of the Hallucination Argument which I
have already refuted, so I will be brief: Macbeth sees a dagger, but not
a real dagger, only an imaginary or hallucinatory dagger. But the
experience is indistinguishable from seeing a real dagger. In the hallucination case, he did not see a real dagger but only a sense datum of a
dagger. But because the two cases are indistinguishable, we should
give the same analysis of each, and therefore we have to say that in the
real, veridical case, he did not see the dagger itself but only a sense
datum of the dagger. We should say that in every case we never see an
ontologically objective phenomenon but only ontologically subjective sense data.

By now, the reader should be able to state the fallacy in the argument quite clearly. In the intentionalistic sense of "see," Macbeth
does not see anything (at least not anything in the dagger line of business; maybe he sees his hand, but he sees nothing in the dagger
department). He experiences a hallucination and we could even say
he "sees" a hallucinatory dagger. But, as we have seen, that is in the
constitutive and not in the intentionalistic sense. In the hallucination
case, *there is no object of the perception.* There is indeed an awareness
and the awareness is identical with itself. Hence, it can be treated as if
the noun naming it were the direct object of "aware of."

9. Shakespeare, William. *Macbeth.* Act II, Scene 1, 33–41.

III. CONSEQUENCES OF THE BAD ARGUMENT FOR THE HISTORY OF PHILOSOPHY

Epistemology from Descartes on was based on a false premise. As I said earlier, it is as if mathematicians had tried to do mathematics on the assumption that there are no numbers. You get some ingenious results in the epistemology, but they are all tragically mistaken.[10]

I have suggested that the three hundred years of epistemology after Descartes was largely, though not entirely, a consequence of the Bad Argument. Specifically, if you think that the only things you ever have perceptual access to are your own subjective experiences, then there is a serious, indeed insoluble, problem of how, on that basis, you can be confident of having knowledge of the existence of an external world. Showing how the acceptance of the Bad Argument largely determined the course of epistemology and, therefore, the course of philosophy, would take an enormous scholarly inquiry into the works of the classic philosophers. I will not attempt to do that, but I will show, by taking a number of cases, how this problem works itself out. Let us start with Hume because he is the clearest case.

Hume tells us that all we can ever perceive are our own subjective impressions and ideas, and the difference between them, he tells us, is one of force and vivacity. Impressions are more forceful, ideas less

---

10. There is something tragic about the massive waste of time involved in the whole tradition of idealism. As it happens, I own Rashdall's first edition copy of Bradley's *Appearance and Reality*. I bought it secondhand at Parker's in Oxford. It is carefully marked with all sorts of comments and annotations in pencil in Rashdall's own hand. Today, probably most readers of this book never heard of Rashdall, though he was a famous Oxford philosopher of his time. Many of you have probably never even heard of Bradley, though he was the most important English philosopher of his era. He was regarded, at least in Britain, as the most important philosopher writing in the English language at that time. So, here are Rashdall and Bradley trying pathetically to work out the intellectual consequences of Hegelian Absolute Idealism, a massive and tragic waste of intellectual effort. I wonder if our intellectual great-grandchildren will find our efforts as futile as we find the efforts of some of our intellectual great-grandparents.

so. If I look at the desk in front of me, all I actually see is not an independently existing (ontologically objective) material object, but rather, my own (ontologically subjective) impression, something going on in my mind. If I close my eyes and think about the table, then what I perceive is a fainter image of my impression, an *idea of the table*. Then he tells us that impressions arise in the soul from unknown causes.[11] Hume indeed supposes that ordinary people reject Naïve Realism about material objects, and assume, with him, that their own perceptions of sensation are of impressions of sensation. But since they also believe that they see tables and chairs, he supposes that they must believe that the tables and chairs are impressions of sensation. He discovers that they also believe that these tables and chairs have a continued and distinct existence, they exist continuously even when we are not perceiving them, and they have an existence distinct from our perception of them. But how can that be the case if our impressions exist only in the mind, when they exist only when they are being perceived? Hume thinks we cannot ask the question whether or not bodies exist, "whether there be body," but rather only "what causes induce us to believe in the existence of body"? The belief in the existence of body is the belief that our own impressions have a continued and distinct existence. This is totally without any rational foundation, but Hume explains in detail why the imagination leads us to this illusory conclusion. His answer is that we have no rational ground for supposing that impressions have a continuous and distinct existence, and, consequently, no ground for supposing that material objects have a continued and distinct existence. These are illusions created in us by the activities of our imagination. The two key sentences in Hume are the claim that all we ever perceive by the senses are "impressions of sensation," and that impressions arise in the soul from unknown causes.

---

11. Hume, David. *A Treatise of Human Nature.*

So much for a brief summary of Hume's theory of perception of material objects. Now suppose he had started out differently. Suppose Hume said that the internal entities in the mind consist of impressions and ideas, where impressions are more forceful than ideas, and these, in the case of impressions of sensation, are caused by the experience of material objects and other features of the external world. The world exists outside our minds and independently of our minds. When Hume says that impressions arise in the mind from unknown causes, that is a stunning claim. Think about my looking at the table right now: I have no doubt where the impression of the table comes from—it is caused by the presence and features of a table. But Hume denies this when he says impressions arise in the soul from unknown causes. In short, once you have adopted Hume's initial assumptions based on the Bad Argument, then the skeptical epistemology pretty much follows.

Always beware of what a philosopher takes for granted as so obvious as to be not worth arguing for. When Hume says that perceptions of the mind divide themselves into impressions and ideas, he just states this as an obvious fact. When he says impressions arise in the soul from unknown causes, he also thinks that that is an obvious fact. But neither is obvious; in fact, on a natural interpretation, they are both false. If perception means "that which we perceive," which at one point he tells us is what he means by it, then we often perceive things that are not impressions, they are chairs, tables, mountains, trees and houses, for example. Furthermore, it is clear what the causes of our impressions are, at least in these cases, the impressions are caused by the actual things we see. But that view, which is the Direct Realist's view, is one that he cannot accept. He thinks it is obviously false, and as I pointed out, I can find only one explicit argument against it.

When we turn to Kant, the effect is even more dramatic. Kant also takes for granted the effects of the Bad Argument. In the very introduction to his *Critique of Pure Reason* (page 22 of the Kemp Smith translation) he refers to "objects, or what is the same thing...the *experience* in which alone, as given objects, they can be known, conform to the concepts." Thus, like Hume, he equates objects and experience.

Kant's whole assumption is that we can never have knowledge of things in themselves. But suppose he had started the *Critique of Pure Reason* by saying, "Typically, in the case of perceptual experiences, we have direct perception of things in themselves, of mountains, trees, chairs, tables, etc." It is hard to imagine how he could have written a *Critique of Pure Reason* if he had started that way. Similarly with Hume, if Hume had said, "impressions of sensation arise in the soul from well-known causes, they are typically caused by the objects and states of affairs in the actual world that we see and otherwise perceive." It would be interesting to see how much of his skeptical arguments would survive if he adopted Direct Realism as his starting point. I have always assumed that his skepticism about causation and induction can be stated without his phenomenalism, though Barry Stroud,[12] in his recent book, objects to this.

Kant's "Copernican Revolution" in metaphysics rests on accepting the conclusion of the Bad Argument. I do not say that he presents the Bad Argument himself; I cannot find it in his work, but he does accept the conclusion that all we can perceive are our own representations. He says,

"If intuition must conform to the constitution of the objects, I do not see how we can know anything of the latter *a priori*; but if the object (as object of the senses) must conform to the constitution of our faculty of intuition, I have no difficulty in conceiving such a possibility... either I must assume that the *concepts*, by means of which I obtain this

---

12. Stroud, Barry. *The Quest for Reality: Subjectivism and the Metaphysics of Color.* Oxford: Oxford University Press, 2000.

determination, conform to the object, or else I assume that the objects, or what is the same thing, that the *experience* in which alone, as given objects, they can be known, conform to the concepts.[13]

What he is saying is that if we assume that objects are given independently of the experience of objects, that is, if we assume some sort of realistic theory of perception, then it would be impossible to know anything a priori about objects. But, if objects just are experiences, then we can know a priori what conditions the mind sets on objects. Thus, we have the possibility of synthetic a priori propositions and the whole Kantian Copernican revolution is such as to create that possibility.

Furthermore, according to Kant, if we adopted the view that ordinary objects are things in themselves, then skepticism would follow. He says,

If we treat outer objects as things in themselves, it is quite impossible to understand how we could arrive at a knowledge of their reality outside us, since we have to rely merely on the representation which is in us. For we cannot be sentient [of what is] outside ourselves, but only [of what is] in us, and the whole of our self-consciousness therefore yields nothing save merely our own determinations.[14]

This is a stunning passage and a stark example of the Bad Argument. If objects such as chairs and tables, trees and stones are things in themselves, then we could never have knowledge of them because our own knowledge is our representations, which are "in us." But why? The only answer in Kant is the Bad Argument. We are aware of our representations and aware of objects, but we are aware of only one sort of thing, and that is in us.

13. Kant, Immanuel. *Critique of Pure Reason*, tr. Norman Kemp Smith. London: Macmillan, 1929, p. 22.
14. Kant, *Critique of Pure Reason*, p. 351.

IV. CONCLUSION

I have, in this chapter, tried to fill in the details that were left out of Chapter 1. The two main claims that I have been making are: First, the Bad Argument is pervasive, it infects both the classical authors from Descartes to Kant and even many contemporary authors. Second, it has been extremely influential in determining the course of epistemology.

Chapter 4

How Perceptual Intentionality Works, Part One

Basic Features, Causation, and Intentional Content

This chapter and the next are the central theoretical chapters of the book. They attempt to explain, at least in part, how the phenomenology of perceptual, especially visual, experience sets conditions of satisfaction. That is a fancy way of saying that they explain how the raw feel of your experience determines what it seems to you that you are perceiving. The problem is not the relatively trivial question, "What fact about you makes it the case that you are seeing something red?", but rather the more philosophically difficult question, "What fact about the phenomenology of your present visual experience makes it necessarily the case that if you have that phenomenology it will seem to you that you are seeing something red?" Why is that question not only more difficult but more important? Because the ontology of perceptual experience is subjective and that ontology must be internally related to the ontologically objective features of the world that constitute the conditions of satisfaction. The raw phenomenology must have features that fix those conditions of satisfaction. The full meaning of this should emerge in what follows.

I will say at the outset that I cannot hope to discuss all or even most of the issues involved. The relations between phenomenology and intentionality are very complex. I mentioned earlier that a change in collateral intentionality can produce a change in the phenomenology. If I believe that it is *my* car, it looks different from type-identical cars. If I believe the house is only a façade as part of a movie set, it looks different from the way it looks if I believe it to be a real house. Beliefs can affect the phenomenology in ways that change the intentional content even though the perceptual stimulus is held constant. Sometimes the phenomenology is inconsistent with what we believe to be the case. In the Müller-Lyer illusion the lines look different lengths, hence the intentionality is that they are different lengths, but I know independently that they are the same length. I will not be concerned with these complexities. From a biological and evolutionary point of view the phenomenology of perception must relate us directly to the world perceived. How does it work? I will be concerned with what I take to be the most basic parts of that question.

I. ANALYTIC PHILOSOPHY AND THE BACKWARD ROAD

Before continuing the analysis I want to situate the discussion within the larger tradition of contemporary and recent philosophy. In large part analytic philosophy has been about the determination of truth conditions. Famously, Frege argued for the distinction between *Sinn* and *Bedeutung* to account for the truth conditions of identity statements such as, "The Evening Star is identical with the Morning Star." Russell argued for a certain application of the predicate calculus to exhibit the truth conditions of sentences containing apparent references to nonexistent objects, such as the sentence, "The present king of France is bald." In a sense, their task was easier than ours because they could rely on the fact that we are all familiar with the conventions of languages, that, for example, by convention certain sounds have certain meanings and references. They could assume that we all understand what it is for something to be red or something to be a king or for something to be France. And in a deeper sense their task was much easier than ours because they could assume what we are trying to explain—namely, that the world is presented to us pre-linguistically, especially in perception, and we then use pre-linguistic presentations to build linguistic representations. We are now trying to examine the pre-linguistic perceptual presentations. The classical empiricists—Locke, Berkeley, Hume, et al.—saw correctly that empirical knowledge expressed linguistically must, in some sense, bottom out in perception. But they never had a satisfactory account of either language or perception. They failed to answer the questions we need to answer in part because of the Bad Argument and in part because they lacked a theory of intentionality. Well, we are not making the Bad Argument and we have a theory of intentionality. It is on that basis that I am proceeding.

In *Intentionality*[1] I extended the analysis of sentences to intentional states generally. Just as we can analyze the truth conditions of the sentence, "The King of France is bald," so we can analyze the truth conditions of the belief that the king of France is bald, the satisfaction conditions of the desire that the king of France should be bald, and the intention to make the king of France bald. We can extend the notion of conditions of satisfaction across intentional states generally. This method of analyzing intentionality is very much a continuation of the traditions of analytic philosophy. You discover features of representations, linguistic or otherwise, whereby they represent states of affairs in the world. In this chapter, we are going to discover that we have to do something that is really quite different from this tradition. We have to go backward from the world to the fixation of the intentional content.[2]

---

1. Searle, John R. *Intentionality: An Essay in the Philosophy of Mind.* Cambridge: Cambridge University Press, 1983.
2. Externalists suppose that they have a causal account of meaning according to which the world determines the intentional content. But a close look shows that their account is

Famously, Russell taught us that there is no backward road from the world to meaning, from references to senses: "...there is no backward road from denotations to meanings, because every object can be denoted by an infinite number of different denoting phrases."[3] But we will discover, in this chapter, that in order that there should be an internal relation between the experience and the type of object it presents, there has to be such a backward road. I hope to make these somewhat dark sayings clear in what follows.

II. THE BOUNDARIES OF THE VISUAL

There are certain constraints that our account has to meet and certain assumptions we have to make, and I want to spell them out at the beginning.

(a) *The account must apply generally to perceiving animals.* It cannot be confined to language possessing adult humans, but it must work for animals and small children. My dog, Tarski, for example, has extremely sophisticated visual perceptions and any philosophy of visual perception has to apply to his experience.

(b) *The account has to respect the phenomenology.* It is just a fact about human phenomenology that we have experiences that we can naturally characterize as having a very rich intentional content. So we do not often say things like "I see

internal throughout. An initial baptism, entirely internally presented, is followed by a causal chain consisting of a transfer of intentional content from one speaker to another. They think the account is external because it relies on indexicals, and they have a mistaken externalist account of indexicals. For detailed discussion, see *Intentionality*, Ch. 9.

3. Russell, Bertrand. "On Denoting," in *Logic and Knowledge,* ed. Robert C. Marsh. London: George Allen & Unwin, 1956, 50.

colors and shapes"; but rather, we say things like "I saw my car in the parking lot," "I saw the Vermeer in the museum," and "I saw that rain clouds were gathering in the northwest" and so on. We can even see negative facts such as, for example, "I saw immediately that there were no people in the classroom" and conditional facts such as "I could see that if he took another step forward he would fall off the edge." All of these statements can be literally true.

(c) Along with respecting the richness of phenomenology with its rich intentional content, *we also have to respect the sheer physics and physiology of the perceptual situation.* All we receive are surface irritations to the retina or stimulations to other peripheral nerve endings, "nerve hits" as Quine called them. How do we get such a rich phenomenology from such a limited physiological input?

(d) Though respecting the phenomenology and the physiology, *we also have to find upper limits to the perceptual intentionality.* I can literally see that there is a red ball in front of me and that it has started raining. But other claims are more problematic. We say things like, "I saw that the man was drunk" or "I saw that she was intelligent," but are these literal reports of visual perception? At one extreme there are straight metaphors. "I see the importance of Kant in the history of Western philosophy" is metaphorical and does not report a visual perception. "I see the red ball" does report a visual perception. What are the upper limits of the *visual* in visual perception? I address this question in the next chapter.

(e) *We take consciousness and intentionality as biologically given.* We assume a neurobiology capable of producing complex forms of consciousness and more problematically we assume that the distinction between the intentional and the nonintentional forms of consciousness is also biologically given. Our question is not, "How does the child or the animal know that vision and touch give them access to the world?" but rather, "How do certain features of conscious experience present certain features of the world?"

III. THE OBJECTIVE AND SUBJECTIVE PERCEPTUAL FIELDS

Our aim in this chapter and the next is to explain the nature of and the relations between the objective and subjective perceptual fields. I will do that, concentrating, as usual, on vision. At the cost of repeating some of the points made in earlier chapters, I will begin by stating some general principles that I think I have already established and that govern the rest of the investigation.

1. Whenever we consciously see anything, the state of affairs that we see causes in us a conscious visual experience

This experience has the usual properties that are so embarrassing to materialistically inclined philosophers. Specifically, the visual experience is ontologically subjective: it exists only insofar as it is experienced by a human or animal subject. Secondly, because it is subjective, it is always qualitative: there is always a certain qualitative character, something that it is like, to have the visual experience. Third, the visual experience does not come in isolation, but it comes as part of a total conscious subjective field and the field has the features of consciousness in general. It makes matters more complex that the visual field itself always occurs as part of the total subjective conscious field including the other perceptual modalities such as tactile and auditory experiences, as well as the stream of thought, moods, emotions, and sundry bodily sensations such as pains. Our main object of investigation in this chapter is the subjective visual experience in the subjective visual field, which is part of the total subjective conscious field.

2. The subjective visual experience has intrinsic intentionality

The visual experience comes with the conditions of satisfaction (in the sense of requirement) built in. There is no way that I can have this present visual experience without it seeming to me that I am seeing San Francisco Bay in the distance and the treetops and houses of North Berkeley in the foreground. The conscious visual experience has an extremely rich conscious intentionality as part of its very content.

3. The subjective visual field has to be sharply distinguished from the objective visual field. The former is an intentional presentation of the latter

The objective visual field is ontologically public and objective, a third-person set of objects and states of affairs that are identified relative to a particular perceiver and his or her point of view. So right now, the objective visual field for me consists of all the objects and states of affairs that I can see under these lighting conditions in my present physiological and psychological state and from this point of view. The subjective visual field is ontologically private, a first-person set of experiences that go on entirely in the head.

4. In the objective visual field, everything is seen or can be seen; in the subjective visual field, nothing is seen nor can be seen

My objective field is defined as the set of objects and states of affairs that are visible from my point of view under these conditions. My subjective visual field, on the other hand, is ontologically subjective, and it exists entirely in my brain. The most important thing to re-emphasize is that *in the subjective visual field, nothing is seen.* This is not because the entities in the subjective visual field are invisible, but rather because their existence is the seeing of objects in the objective visual field. One thing you cannot see when you see anything is your seeing of that thing. And this holds whether or not the case is a good case or a bad case, whether it is veridical or hallucinatory, because in the hallucinatory case you do not see anything. And in particular, you do not see the hallucinatory seeing. To think otherwise, to think that the entities in the subjective visual field are themselves seen, is to commit the Bad Argument. It is, as I have argued earlier, the disaster from which a large number of the disasters of Western philosophy over the past four centuries result.

I actually believe that if this point had been appreciated, not just about vision but about perception in general, from the seventeenth century on, the entire history of Western philosophy would have been different. Many truly appalling mistakes—from Descartes' Representative Theory of Perception all the way through to Kant's Transcendental Idealism and beyond—would have been avoided if everybody understood you cannot see or otherwise perceive any-thing in the subjective perceptual field.

5. Perception is "transparent"

The description of the objective visual field and the subjective visual field will typically be exactly the same, the same words in the same order. This is for the, by now I hope, obvious reason that the subjective visual field is an intentional presentation of the objective visual field. So I say, speaking of what I literally see, "I see San Francisco Bay with the Peninsula on the left and Marin on the right." If I want to speak only of my visual experience, I would say, "I have a visual experience, which is exactly as if I were seeing San Francisco Bay with the Peninsula on the left and Marin on the right." (In ordinary English, to isolate the visual experience, we would typically use the word "seem" and say "I seem to see San Francisco Bay," etc. But "seem" in these sentences has a scope ambiguity. So, "I seem to see San Francisco" can be interpreted as either "It seems to me that I see San Francisco" or "I have a visual experience which is exactly as if I were seeing San Francisco." To avoid these ambiguities, I specify the visual experience explicitly and do not use the word "seem.")

Incidentally, it is worth pointing out that the same parallelism exists in the structure of human action. My raising my arm can be described as either an objective event—my arm went up—or as a subjective intentional phenomenon—"What were you doing?" "I was trying to raise my arm." We can carve off the subjective from the objective because the subjective event is my intention-in-action, my "trying." The objective event is the causal effect of my trying, my arm going up. Action is exactly parallel to perception with different directions of fit and different directions of causation. In action, the objective element is my physical arm going up, and it occurs as caused by the subjective element, my consciously trying to raise my arm. In perception, the objective element is the state of affairs perceived, and it causes the subjective element, the conscious perceptual experience.

6. The intentional object of your perception is its intentional cause

It is a basic Background disposition of conscious animals like ourselves that we take the intentional object of perception to be the thing causing the perceptual experience. This is perhaps most obvious in cases where you know nothing else about the object of your perception, you at least know that it caused the perceptual experiences. Think of bumping into something in the dark or suddenly hearing a loud noise or smelling an unpleasant smell or seeing an unexpected flash appear on the window. In all of these cases I am assuming that you do not know what it is that you are perceiving, in the sense that you cannot identify it, but in every case you do know that the object of your perception is whatever caused the perceptual experience. This is a crucial point for the argument of this chapter. Other things equal, *whenever you consciously perceive anything, you take the cause of your perceptual experience to be its object.* This principle applies both to the perception of individual objects, as for example when you see your spouse, and the perception of general features, as, for example, when you see something red. I am talking of course of intentional causation, that is, the cause of the specific intentional content that you have is the intentional object of the perception. So in the present case, the cause of my visual experience of San Francisco Bay is San Francisco Bay. In order for my seeing San Francisco Bay to occur, there is a very complex non-intentional causal story about the neurobiology of vision, and without that causal sequence the perceiving cannot occur. For example, the causal story involves feedback mechanisms between V1 (Visual Area 1) and the LGN (Lateral Geniculate Nucleus). But V1 and the LGN are not part of the intentional contents nor are they intentional objects. There is a very complex non-intentional causal story, which enables the intentionality to work.

We do not hold a *theory* that the thing that causes our conscious experiences is the thing we are perceiving, we simply take it for granted. It is a biologically given Background presupposition. I have heard philosophers claim that we do not experience the causation in visual perception. Nothing could be further from the truth. There is no way I can have these visual experiences without having them as experiences of the thing causing the experiences themselves. And what goes for me goes for my dog and other consciously perceiving animals with a perceptual apparatus relevantly like ours.

IV. THE STRUCTURE OF THE SUBJECTIVE VISUAL FIELD

In this and the next sections, I will present some of the central formal features of perceptual content and conditions of satisfaction. They are formal in the sense that they are not specific to any particular content but apply to any content at all that presents, for example, a color or a shape.

The objective visual field typically contains enduring material objects and states of affairs. In the subjective visual field nothing is enduring, everything is a temporary and fleeting process, and the whole thing shuts down whenever you close your eyes. The subjective visual field consists of visual processes not permanent objects.

The fact that the processes in the subjective visual field, the experiences, have intentionality has two important consequences mentioned earlier in Chapter 2: all seeing is *seeing as* and all seeing is *seeing that*. I will consider each in order.

Seeing As and Aspectual Shape. Because presentational visual intentionality is a subspecies of representation, and because all representation is under aspects, the visual presentations will always present their conditions of satisfaction under some aspects and not others. So, for example, I see the table in front of me from a certain point of view, and I see only certain aspects of the table. I see its surface and side from this angle. What is true of this trivial case is true generally.

Seeing That. Because all perceptual intentionality sets conditions of satisfaction, and because a condition is always a condition that such and such obtains, the content of perceptual intentionality is always that such and such. So, for example, one never just sees an object. One sees an object in front of one—directly in front or to the left or above or below. In every visual experience some total state of affairs is presented. The phenomenology disguises this from us by giving the impression that visual experience is a simple relation to an object. It is not. It is always a total state of affairs, and this follows from the intentionality of visual experience.

In earlier writings I said that perception always has a propositional content. This is true but misleading to philosophers for two reasons. One is that many of them hold the absurdly mistaken view that propositional attitudes consist of relations to propositions. In a variation on the Bad Argument, they suppose the proposition must be the object of the perception. And, secondly, they suppose these propositions are something "abstract." In order to prevent these two misunderstandings, I have stopped using the notion of proposition in the analysis of perception and just say that the perceptual experience has as content the *condition* that such-and-such is the case. "Condition" in the sense of requirement means the same as "proposition" (because a condition is always a condition that such-and-such), but I hope it prevents the misunderstandings.

V. THE HIERARCHICAL STRUCTURE OF VISUAL PERCEPTION

These two features, when properly understood in relation to the phenomenology of human visual experience, have important consequences. Perceptual experiences are typically hierarchically structured. I have repeated over and over that the visual experience for normal humans is extremely rich in its intentional content. I do not just see colors and shapes, but I see cars and houses, and indeed, I do not just see cars and houses, I see my car and my house, for example. Now, how is all of that possible? It is possible because *the rich intentional content requires a hierarchical structure of lower perceptual features, all of which are part of the content of the seeing as.* The notion of "seeing as" already implicitly suggests a hierarchy because in order to see X as Y, you have to see X, the lower order in the hierarchy, and you have to see it as Y, the higher order.

Many years ago Arthur Danto introduced the idea of a basic action.[4] I am not concerned with his original intentions, but I find the notion useful and the way I use it is: a basic action is anything you can do without intending to do anything else by-way-of which or by-means-of which you do it. So for me raising my arm is a basic action, I do not have to do anything else, I just raise it. But writing this book is not a basic action. In order to do it intentionally, I have to intend to do a whole lot of other things. Because of the formal isomorphism of the structure of perception and action, we can extend the notion of basic action to basic perception. A basic perception is any perception of an object or feature that you can have without perceiving anything else by way of which you perceive it.

Let us go through this with a simple example. As I said earlier, I do not typically just see colors and shapes, I see a black car. I do not just see any black car, I see a black 911 Carrera 4. And I do not just see any such token of a type, I see my car. *At each level, the perception of the higher level requires a perception of the lower level.* For me, seeing the object as my car requires seeing it as a specific kind of car, and that in turn requires seeing it as having a certain sort of shape and size and color. In each case, the perception of the object as having the higher level feature requires perception of the lower level features.

Eventually, if you carry through the steps, you reach rock bottom. You reach a set of properties which can be perceived without perceiving anything else by way of which you perceive them. I propose to introduce a technical term to name such properties. *All perception requires Basic Perceptual Properties or Basic Perceptual Features,* where the hierarchy of the higher level structure bottoms out in features that do not require the perception of anything else in order to be perceived. *A basic perceptual feature is a feature you can perceive without perceiving any other feature by way of which you perceive it.* The color

4. Danto, Arthur C. "Basic Actions," *American Philosophical Quarterly* 2, no. 2 (1965): 141–48.

and shape of the car are basic perceptual features in this sense, but being a car or being my car are not basic perceptual features. Basic perceptual features are ontologically objective. There are such things, such as the color and shape of the car, that are perceivable by anyone. Corresponding to the ontologically objective basic perceptual features are the subjective visual experiences of these features. A crucial question we will address in this chapter is: How does the phenomenology of those experiences set basic perceptual features as their conditions of satisfaction?

I think, intuitively, the idea of the basic perceptual features and the corresponding hierarchical structure of visual experience is clear. But it is not easy to state it precisely, and I have so far not succeeded in doing so to my satisfaction. Intuitively, both color and shape are basic, but, typically, you cannot perceive one without the other. So which is more basic? A basic perceptual feature is one you can perceive without perceiving any other feature by way of which you perceive it. But colors and shapes are perceived together, so they seem equally basic. I do not have a solution to this problem, but in what follows I am going to rely on the intuitive idea that perception is hierarchically structured and that the hierarchies bottom out in the most basic features. Maybe the right way to deal with the problem of color and shape is to think of the basic features in these cases as colored shapes.

In order that the subjective perceptual field should be rich enough to fix the intentional content, there has to be, for each of the basic perceptual features of objects, a subjective correlate of that basic visual property. This means that in the subjective visual field there must be conscious processes corresponding to color, line, angle, shape, spatial relations, and even temporal relations. But how can that be? There is nothing, for example, in the visual field that is literally red and nothing in the visual field that is literally round. Redness and roundness are objective features of objects that can be literally seen, but to repeat the point made over and over: nothing in the subjective field is literally seen. I think this point is correct and powerful; but, all the same, I want to insist that if we are going to understand visual perception, then, for example, when I look at a red ball, we have to understand that the redness of the ball has a psychological correlate in my subjective visual field and so does the roundness. I now turn to the question of how it works.

VI. HOW DO THE PHENOMENOLOGICAL FEATURES OF THE SUBJECTIVE VISUAL FIELD DETERMINE THE CONDITIONS OF SATISFACTION OF THE VISUAL EXPERIENCE?

This is not a trivial question, and I have at various times in my life firmly believed propositions that I now think are false. I think the best way for me to try to answer it is to go through the steps that led me to my present position. I hope this is more than autobiographical self-indulgence. I think anybody who thinks hard about these issues is likely to go through something like the steps I went through.

Stages in the Development of My Own Thinking

Stage One, Intentionality 1983. Disquotation. When I wrote *Intentionality,* I did not think there was a substantive question of how *intrinsic* perceptual intentionality fixes conditions of satisfaction. There is a philosophical question about how the sentence, "There is a red ball there," fixes truth conditions. The sentence has derived intentionality and we need to explain how and from what exactly it is derived. But if I literally see that there is a red ball there, my visual experience has intrinsic, and not derived, intentionality. And there seems no answer to the question how it fixes the conditions of satisfaction other than to say it is already intrinsic to the experience that it sets those conditions:

it could not be that type of experience if it did not have those conditions. The only characterization of the relation between the intrinsic intentionality and the state of affairs is the trivial one of disquotation. The only reason that we can give why this experience fixes the conditions of satisfaction that there is a red ball there is that this experience is precisely one of seeming to see that there is a red ball there, in the sense that it is satisfied only if the presence and redness of the ball are causing this very visual experience.[5]

On this disquotational conception there cannot be any question of how the raw phenomenology fixes the conditions of satisfaction, because the raw phenomenology *just is* the presentation of those conditions of satisfaction. With sentences and pictures there is a gulf between the object and its conditions of satisfaction. The gulf is crossed in the case of sentences by the meaning of the sentence, in the case of pictures by the representational features of the pictures; but in the case of conscious perceptual experiences, the raw experience allows for no gulf between the experience and the determination of the conditions of satisfaction, because the conditions of satisfaction (in the sense of requirement) just are part of the experience.

Stage Two, Intrinsic Features. Stage One seems dissatisfying because the visual experience is an event in the world like any other. There ought to be a question of how it relates to its conditions of satisfaction, and that question has to be answered non-intentionalistically. A priori it seems there must be basic non-intentional features of the visual experience that fix the conditions of satisfaction. Contrast the visual experience with the sentence. The sentence, "There is a red ball there," fixes the condition of satisfaction because of the conven-

---

5. The traditional notion of disquotation is that in stating the truth conditions of a statement, one simply drops the quotation marks on the right-hand side. Thus "snow is white" is true if and only if snow is white. The sentence on the left-hand side has the quotation marks. On the right-hand side these are dropped, hence "disquotation." I have extended that notion in cases where we have a commonality but without quotation marks.

tions attaching to the sentence that determine its meaning, and its meaning determines those conditions of satisfaction. The meaning is attached to something that lacks intrinsic intentionality, the sentence as a syntactical phenomenon. In the case of the visual experience there is no convention, but there must be some other feature of the visual experience that fixes those conditions of satisfaction. Stage One is right that the conditions of satisfaction are internal to the perceptual experience in a way that they are not internal to sentences or pictures. "Internal" means that the experience could not be that experience if it did not have those conditions of satisfaction. But, all the same, there has to be a question: How does it work? How is it that that particular experience can have those conditions of satisfaction internal to it? And it will not do to say that it just does. Of course it just does. The question is how.

Stage Three, the Hierarchy and Basic Features. An investigation in Stage Two reveals that visual experiences are indeed hierarchical, and the hierarchy in the subjective visual field corresponds to a perceptually accessible hierarchy in the ontologically objective world. So in order to see that it is my car, I have to see that it is a specific kind of car; and in order to see that it is that kind of car, I have to see certain colors and shapes. Objectively, in order to be my car, it must be a certain kind of car, and to be that kind of car, it must have certain colors and shapes. This hierarchy leads to the doctrine of basic perceptual features and basic perceptual experiences. The basic perceptual features are those that you can perceive without perceiving anything else by way of which you perceive them, and the basic perceptual experiences are experiences of the basic perceptual features.

This is an important result not only in its own right but also because it shows there is an ambiguity in Stage Two. The requirement that there be basic perceptual experiences is not the same requirement that these features be specified nonintentionalistically. The basic perceptual experiences still could be characterizable only in terms of their intentionality. Even given a hierarchical structure of perception, disquotation might still be the right approach.

Stage Four, the Intentionality of the Nonintentional. To say that the basic perceptual experiences are intrinsically intentional is an unsatisfactory answer to our question because of the point of Stage Two, namely the visual experience is an event in the world like any other, so there must be some features of that event that fix conditions, and those features must be specified non-intentionalistically. Why? Because otherwise the account is circular and does not explain anything. That is, it is true that the experiences of the basic features have intrinsic intentionality, but those very intrinsic intentional features are intentional *in virtue of* something, and that something has now got to be specified, and it cannot be specified simply disquotationally. That they are basic and that they are intrinsically intentional seemed to me to imply that there is nothing more to be said. But that is a mistake. The point that the basic visual features have intrinsic intentionality does not by itself answer the question, How do they get the specific intentionality that they have? That is the question I now intend to answer.

As I said earlier, traditionally analytic philosophy examines the meaning of sentences in such a way as to explain their truth conditions. Because the meaning is conventional, there is no internal connection between the sentence and its condition of satisfaction. That very sentence could be used to mean anything. But because there is an internal connection in the case of conscious perceptual experiences between the character of the experience and the condition of satisfaction, we must explain that internal connection; and the only way that we can explain it is to go backwards from the world to the representation (or in this case, presentation), otherwise we cannot get the internal connection. I know this sounds mysterious, but I will explain the mystery shortly.

VII. MY CURRENT VIEW

Stage Five, How Things Are and What Experiences They Cause. We need to make the question precise. The question is not the old philosophers' question, "How is intentionality possible at all?" I do not think it is a meaningful philosophical question. It is like other philosophical questions we have abandoned. How is life possible in a world of nonliving matter? How is consciousness possible in a world of unconscious matter? How is intentionality possible in a world of unrepresenting matter? These are not philosophical questions. The first is being answered by evolutionary biology, and I think the second and third questions about consciousness and intentionality are being answered by neurobiology. The question, "How is intentionality possible at all?" is answered by showing, for example, how it is possible for an animal to feel thirsty. In large part we know the answer to that.

The question we are addressing is the more specific question, "How do specific features of the ontologically subjective visual field present features of the objective visual field as their conditions of satisfaction?" There are two traditional answers to our question, both of which are wrong. The first is resemblance. The idea, common to philosophers from Locke and Descartes right through Wittgenstein's *Tractatus*, is that representation is explained by a resemblance relation or isomorphism between the representing and the represented. On Wittgenstein's account there is an isomorphism between the *Satz* and the *Tatsache*. The sentence represents by resembling the fact. The fact consists of an arrangement of objects. The sentence consists of an arrangement of names. And the sentence represents the fact because there is a picturing relation between the sentence and the fact. In the case of perception, according to the Representative Theory, we perceive a picture in our mind and the picture represents an object in the world by resembling it. Quite apart from the fact that this commits the Bad Argument in the case of perception, it is important to see that the explanation does not work in either case. Suppose that we ignore the Bad Argument and we simply say that the visual experience is itself red, and it represents red objects in the world because it resembles them. I have even heard some philosophers say that the visual experience is red in a different sense of red from the sense in which the object is red. Well let us suppose that there is some sense in which the visual experience is red or the visual experience is square and represents red and square things by resembling them. Would these resemblances between the visual experiences and their objects explain how the visual experiences have the objects as their conditions of satisfaction? They have no explanatory power whatever. The fact that there are two resembling entities does not make one a representation of the other in either perception or language. Who sees the resemblance? My left hand and my right hand resemble each other as much as any two objects in the world, but the one is not a picture or statue or representation of the other. Resemblance by itself explains nothing. It has no explanatory power. Philosophers mistakenly take it as explanatory because they assimilate intentionality to pictures; and pictures, such as the picture on my driver's license, do in fact represent by a combination of causation and resemblance. But it is important to notice that the resemblance relation is not the explanation of depiction, but rather it is the tip of an iceberg of cognitive capacities that enable us to interpret the one as a representation of the other. Two resembling objects by themselves do not in any way explain representation, much less the intentional presentation of visual perception.

But what about causation? By itself causation has no explanatory power either. Let us suppose that a certain sort of experience is caused by red objects. That is indeed the case, but by itself that does not explain why the experience has red objects as the condition of satisfaction. Roughly speaking, anything can cause anything. Suppose seeing red objects invariably caused in me a painful sensation. This would not make the painful sensation into an intentional state that had redness as its condition of satisfaction. If we are going to show how the raw phenomenological character of the subjective visual experience presents its conditions of satisfaction, neither resemblance nor causation by itself is going to do the job. And I think in fact it is something of a historical scandal in philosophy that both of these have been routinely appealed to as explanations of intentionality. These mistakes date from the Representative Theory of Perception of the seventeenth century right up to the causal theories of reference in the twentieth and twenty-first centuries. I think one of the weakest features of contemporary and recent philosophy is the appeal to "causal chains" to try to explain semantics. These "causal chains" have no explanatory power whatsoever. I have criticized the causal theories of reference and meaning in *Intentionality* (Chapters 8 and 9), and I will not repeat the criticisms here.

In order to explain why neither resemblance nor causation does the job of explaining intentionality, we need to say more about what an explanation requires. We are trying to explain, for example, why it is internal to *this very subjective perceptual experience* that, if satisfied, it must be a case of seeing something red. The explanation must be stated in terms that are not themselves intentionalistic and must give sufficient conditions. It must show why if you have this experience, it must be a case of seeming to see something red. Why does this very perceptual experience present red as its conditions of satisfaction? It is indeed a necessary condition of seeing something red that the experience must be caused by a red object; but that does not answer the question we are trying to answer, which is not what third-person objective fact is necessary for it to be the case that I see a red object, but rather what fact about the first-person subjective experience makes it the case that it is necessarily a presentation of a red object. What non-intentional fact about this very experience, whether veridical or not, makes it a case for me of seeming to see a red object? We are not trying to give necessary conditions, because of course different sensory modalities can give access to the same property and in the case of hallucination the same phenomenological type of event can be caused by something other than its veridical type of object. I can both see that the object is round and feel that it is round and I can have a visual hallucination of seeing something round.

The sentence, "There is a red object in front of me" has its conditions of satisfaction by convention. That very sentence could have meant something different. But the very visual experience's conditions of satisfaction are that there is a red object in front of me must have those conditions of satisfaction by necessity. It must be essential to its being that very experience that it has those conditions of satisfaction. How does that work?

In what follows, I want to answer this question by exploring the relations for the basic features between *how things are, the qualitative character of the subjective perceptual experiences,* and the *causal relations between them.* This will enable us to explore the relation between how things are and how they look. The hypothesis I want to explore is that the explanation of how the qualitative features of the visual experience in the case of the basic features present the conditions of satisfaction that they do, is that there is a systematic relation between the property of being F and the property of *being able to cause a certain sort of experience.* In ordinary speech that experience would be described as "looking F." But looking F will not solve our problem, because looking F normally means looking *to be F.* You understand "looking F" only if you understand "being F." I will illustrate these points beginning with the example of color.

Color is a bit tricky because of such phenomena such as spectrum inversion and color constancy, and we will get to those issues in the next chapter. Let us now examine our visual experience of the red ball. Is the visual experience itself red? Emphatically, visual experiences are not colored. Why not? Colors are observable to all, and visual experiences are not. The color red emits photons of about 6500 angstrom units and the visual experience emits nothing. So it is wrong to think of the visual experience as itself colored. Also, to think that visual experiences are colored is almost inevitably to commit the Bad Argument because one has to ask who is seeing the color.

Colors are objects of perceptual experiences, but they are not themselves features of the perceptual experiences. Let us explore the implications of this. If you close your eyes and cover your eyes with your hand, you will have in your visual field a set of experiences that naïvely one might describe as yellow patches against a black background. Why is this a natural description? First, the experience you have is *something like* seeing yellow patches against a black background. And, second, for example, if a doctor manipulating your visual system electronically produced a change, we would know what it would mean for him to produce the change that you would describe as green patches against a black background, or orange patches against a black background. All the same, to repeat, there is nothing that I am experiencing that is literally black or yellow, for the reasons I stated earlier. But what this thought experiment suggests is that when I see something red, corresponding to the red object in the objective visual field is something in the subjective visual field that carries that intentional content, red. Why does it carry that content? How exactly does it do it? The next two points are the crucial points in this entire discussion. First, for something *to be red* in the ontologically objective world is for it to be capable of *causing ontologically subjective visual experiences like this*. The fact of its redness consists at least in part in its causal capacity (with the usual qualifications about normal conditions and normal observers) to cause this sort of ontologically subjective visual experience. There is an internal relation between the fact of being red and the fact of causing this sort of experience. What does it mean to say that the relation is "internal"? It means it could not be that color if it were not systematically related in that way to experiences like this. Second, for something to be the object of a perceptual experience is for it to be experienced as the cause of the experience. If you put these two points together, you get the result that the perceptual experience necessarily carries the existence of a red as its condition of satisfaction. How? Your Background disposition, biologically given, is to presuppose that the object you are perceiving is whatever caused the perception and the "object" in question, a token of the color red, consists (at least in part) in the ability to cause experiences like this. The presence of the object is a sufficient, not a necessary, condition for causing this sort of experience because in the case of indiscriminable hallucination the experience is caused by something other than its veridical object.

We are assuming that the animal has conscious intentionality as a biological given in exactly the same way that it has conscious thirst and hunger as biological forms of intentionality. The question is, how does the perceptual intentionality get the content that it has? The answer I am proposing for the basic perceptual experiences is that the experience of having this conscious visual experience necessarily carries the intentionality that it does because the feature in question is experienced as caused by its object and its object is precisely constituted (at least in part[6]) by its ability to cause this type of experience.

If perceptual experiences, human or animal, could be conscious of what they are and what is going on when they occur and could talk, they would say, "I am the seeing of the thing F that is causing me to exist as a conscious experience. And every conscious perceptual experience, whether veridical or not, is experienced as a perception of the thing causing the experience. And I am the seeing of it *as F* because its being F consists in its ability to cause experiences like me."

One of the worst features of traditional philosophical accounts of perception is the general failure to see that conscious perceptual experi-

6. Why do I have to keep saying "at least in part"? Because as we find out more about the physics, we can define things in terms of features other than the perceptual features. Color can (to some extent) be defined in terms of photon emissions and lines in terms of their geometrical properties.

ences are experienced as causal throughout. You experience the object of your perception as causing the perceptual experience. The form of the causation is intentional causation. I am not sure why this mistake is so pervasive, but I think it must have something to do with Hume's influence. Hume tried to teach us that we never experience causation. I have argued[7] that we experience causation pretty much all of our waking life. Whenever we perceive or act consciously, we experience the causal connection; and, to repeat, the form of the causation is intentional causation. In the case of action, the intention-in-action is a causal presentation of a bodily movement. In the case of perception, the state of affairs perceived causes the very perceptual experience that presents that state of affairs as its condition of satisfaction.

The point about red is generalizable to other colors. A visual experience is not literally red or blue or green, but nonetheless it necessarily *presents* red or blue or green as its condition of satisfaction because for something to be red or blue or green is precisely for it to be capable of causing this sort of experience. The visual experience has a certain qualitative character, and that qualitative character is correctly described as determining the intentional content that the experience is one where something looks red, precisely because being red consists in being able to cause visual experiences that have this character. Given that an object is red, what fact about it makes it red? The fact that makes it red is, at least in part, that it is capable of causing a certain sort of experience. So you get an internal set of relations of something being red and it causing a certain sort of visual experience. The non-intentional characterization of the visual experience is simply that it has this sort of qualitative character. *That qualitative character fixes red as the conditions of satisfaction because (in part) the essence of redness is the ability to cause experiences that have this character, and any perceptual experience is experienced as having its cause as its object.*

7. Searle, John R. *Intentionality.* Chapter 5.

There is a certain ontologically objective qualitative character in the world, let us call it "red." There is also a certain ontologically subjective qualitative character of my experience, to avoid any Bad Argument, let us call it "Glog." Now why should there be any connection at all between Glog and red? After all, even if the red object caused Glog, anything can cause anything. So what is the connection supposed to be? The beginning of an answer is to say that there is a connection because "red" is defined as the ability to cause Glog (with the usual qualifications about normal conditions and normal observers). And the object of Glog is defined as the cause of Glog. This point is generalizable to all colors. For an object to be a certain color is simply for it to be capable of causing certain sorts of experiences in normal perceivers under normal lighting conditions.

Once that point is accepted, we can now introduce an intermediary concept, the concept of looking. Once red is defined in the way that I have specified, then for something to be red is for it to look red to normal observers under normal conditions. But it is important to emphasize that this, by itself has no explanatory power at all, because looking red just means looking *to be* red, looking *as if it were* red. And that means that looking red is parasitic on being red, and consequently cannot be used to explain it. The explanatory force *comes in* when we say that for it to look red to normal observers under normal conditions is for the object to cause visual experiences of type Glog.

The visual experience of type Glog does not present red just because it is caused by red. That is not the story. The story rather is that the visual experience presents red because it is the essence of something *being red* that it is capable of causing *these sorts of experiences*, and the presentational intentionality of perceptual experience always has the cause of the experience as its object. The causal relation by itself is not enough; the specificity of the intentional content has to be determined by the essential features of the visual experience in question, *otherwise that intentional content will not fix that specificity.* (To repeat a point made earlier, suppose that red objects invariably caused in me a painful sensation. This fact would not make the painful sensation into an intentional state that had redness as its condition of satisfaction.)

What I am saying must apply to animals like my dog, Tarski, as much as they apply to human beings. If you watch a dog or other higher animal engaged in some intense activity, such as digging for a bone or chasing a cat, you see that the whole experience is causal throughout and involves a complex set of coordination of perception in action. The dog has a visual experience as caused by the cat that he is chasing, and he coordinates his bodily movements—more causation—to match what he is getting from his visual and olfactory experiences.

I think this account applies generally to the so-called secondary qualities. For something to taste sweet is for it to be able to cause gustatory sensations like this one. It is difficult to develop the argument in detail because most of our vocabulary for describing the qualities perceived in taste and smell derive from the types of objects tasted or smelled. So, for example, "it smells like gasoline" or "tastes like red wine" typically describe the sensations and the experiences in terms of their typical causes. Nonetheless, I think the account works for them as well. For something to smell like gasoline is (1) for it to cause this sort of experience and (2) that this sort of experience is typically caused by smelling gasoline. But the difference between these cases and the earlier cases is that being red wine, or being gasoline, does not consist even in part in being able to cause these sorts of experiences.

VIII. THE ROLE OF PRESENTATIONAL INTENTIONAL CAUSATION

We can now state the same points from the point of view of the causal character of the perceptual experience. It is a Background presupposition of all conscious perceptual experience that you take it for granted that what you are perceiving is what causes your subjective perceptual experience. Think of the examples I mentioned earlier. For example, when you hear a strange and unexpected sound, you take it for granted that the auditory event in the subjective perceptual field was caused by a sound in the objective perceptual field. Similarly, when you smell a strange smell, or run your hand along the top of the desk and feel the smoothness of the surface, in every case you simply take it for granted that the subjective experience is caused not by just *any* objective state of affairs but by the *very one* that you are perceiving. Now let us apply this lesson to the perception of the red object. You look at an object in the objective visual field, and you have a certain subjective experience in the subjective visual field. We have been calling this visual experience Glog. But your Background presupposition is that what you are seeing is what caused Glog. Now, what makes the subjective perceptual experience into a presentation of red is simply that red consists precisely, at least in part, in the ability to cause subjective perceptual experiences like Glog.

I now think we have satisfied our requirements at least for the case of color and other so-called secondary qualities. We have shown how the characterization of the perceptual experience in non-intentional terms gives us sufficient (and in this case necessary) conditions for it being, when veridical, a perception of red. The internal connection between the experience and its object is guaranteed by the fact that the object essentially, so to speak, by definition consists in, at least in part, the ability to cause that type of experience. That is what I meant when I said we would go backwards from reality to representation, rather than follow the tradition of analytic philosophy that goes from representation to reality. In the sentence "There is a red object in front of me" the conditions of satisfaction are determined by the meaning of the sentence, and that meaning is imposed on sounds and marks that are not intrinsically intentional. But in the visual experience reported by, "I see that there is a red object in front of me," the visual experience is intrinsically intentional. It could not be that visual experience if it did not have that visual intentionality. It gets the visual intentionality that it has by a backward road from the object to the presentation because for something to be a red object is precisely for to be able to cause visual experiences of this type. (More about this in Section X.)

IX. THE PRIMARY QUALITIES

So far this gives us an account of the secondary qualities. What about the so-called primary qualities? I will discuss depth perception in the next chapter, but let us immediately consider such two-dimensional primary qualities as line and shape. Though I think the connection is not as tight as it is in the case of the secondary qualities, even for shapes and lines there is a conceptual connection, a necessary connection, between the features of the object and its ability to cause certain sorts of experiences. Part of what it is for an object to be a straight line or to be a circle is to be able to cause this sort of experience. In ordinary English, we would say that for an object to be a straight line or a circle is, at least in part, for it to "look like this." That is right, but it is important to re-emphasize that "look like this" has to be explained in terms of the character of the visual experience, and not conversely.

The primary qualities are made complicated by the fact that we have what we think of as independent means for establishing the straightness of the line or circularity of the circle. For something to be a circle, for example, is to have all its points on the surface equidistant from a common center. That is correct. But I think all of those notions in turn have a conceptual and necessary connection between how things look and how they really are. So the general principle is that intentional content of the basic perceptual experiences is fixed by the *combination* of the causal relation and the features of the visual experience construed non-intentionalistically. Ontologically objective features of the basic perceptual features of the world cause visual experiences whose character is partly definitional of the feature of the world. A straight line is one that looks like this and "looks like this" implies that it is capable of causing this sort of visual experience. This point holds for the primary as well as for the secondary qualities.

Think of the problem from a designer point of view. Suppose you are God or evolution and you are designing organisms capable of coping with their environment in spectacularly successful ways. First, you create an environment that has objects with shapes, sizes, movements, etc. Furthermore, you create an environment with differential light reflectances. Then you create organisms with spectacularly rich visual capacities. Within certain limits, the whole world is open to their visual awareness. But now you need to create a specific set of perceptual organizations where specific visual experiences are internally tied to specific features of the world, such that being those features involves the capacity to produce those sorts of experiences. Reality is not dependent on experience, but conversely. The *concept* of the reality in question already involves the causal capacity to produce certain sorts of experiences. So the reason that these experiences present red objects is that the very fact of being a red object involves a capacity to produce this sort of experience. Being a straight line involves the capacity to produce this other sort of experience. The upshot is that organisms cannot have these experiences without it seeming to them that they are seeing a red object or a straight line, and that "seeming to them" marks the intrinsic intentionality of the perceptual experience.

Given that we have everywhere discovered a mirror-image isomorphism between perception and action, we should look for a similar isomorphism in the structure of intentional action. What fact described non-intentionalistically about the experience of acting when I raise my arm gives it the condition of satisfaction that it does?

And we found in the case of perception that it is of the essence of something being red that it causes a certain sort of experience, so it is of the essence of being this sort of experience that it causes a certain sort of bodily movement. This intention-in-action is internally related to the bodily movement because it could not be that very sort of experience if it did not typically cause that very sort of bodily movement. Of course one has to add all the usual qualifications about normal behavior under normal conditions, but the internal connection remains the same in perception and action with opposite directions of fit and directions of causation. The difference is that the intention-in-action can only be specified in terms of its intentional content, for example, trying to raise my arm. The perceptual experience has a non-intentional characterization of its intentional content precisely because the intentional content is a result of the "Backward Road," a topic to which I now turn.

X. THE BACKWARD ROAD

Generalizing Russell's argument from language to the mind generally, we can say that he taught us that there is no backward road from objects or types of objects to intentional contents because the same object or type of object can be referred to by way of an indefinite range of different types of intentional contents. But where the basic perceptual features are concerned, there is a backward road, and indeed there must be a backward road, from type of basic feature to type of perceptual experience. The reason is that the basic perceptual features are defined, in part, precisely by their ability to cause certain sorts of perceptual experiences, where those experiences therefore necessarily have that feature as their "referent," their condition of satisfaction.

And this is not a trivial result because it preserves an important insight of traditional empiricism that has tended to become lost in subsequent philosophy, even in subsequent empiricist philosophy. Traditionally, empiricists thought that there is an essential connection between how things really are and how we perceive them to be. They did this as part of their theory of knowledge. Knowledge of reality can be based on sensory experiences only if there is such a connection. Of course, trivially, we can make the connection simply by saying, "Well, a veridical perception requires that things perceived be such and such," but of course we have packed success into that claim by using the word 'veridical.'" Our question now is: Is there an essential connection between the character of things in the world and the character of our experience? I have answered that question by saying that for the basic perceptual features, there must be such a connection because being the basic perceptual feature in question consists, in part, in its ability to cause a certain sort of perceptual experience.

XI. A POSSIBLE OBJECTION

There is an objection to the entire account that may be serious. Here is how it goes: the account is either trivial or false. You are assuming that Glog is in fact caused by red objects. But that makes the account trivial. The question is: how does Glog get the feature that it seems to be caused by red objects? And it is trivial to say that it seems to be caused by red objects because it really is caused by red objects. This assumes what we are trying to explain and so has no explanatory value.

But if we do not make that assumption, then the account is false. Anything can cause anything, and Glog might be caused by anything. Suppose there is a brain in a vat rigged up so that a certain electronic stimulus to the poor brain gives it the impression of seeing something red. You cannot say on the one hand that it really is seeing the stimulus. (Certain causal theorists are forced to say this.) And you cannot say that on the other hand it really is the case of seeing red because it is a persistent hallucination. Another way to put the objection is to ask, how does it come about the being red consists in the ability to cause Glog? From whose point of view does this equation occur?

I am not sure I can answer this objection, but I am pretty sure there is something wrong with it. It treats the causation in question as ordinary billiard ball causation, and we are talking about intentional causation throughout. Intentional causation, like all intentionality, is normative. If you have a belief, the content of the belief has to determine under what conditions it is true or false. Similarly, if you have a desire, the content of the desire has to determine under what conditions it is satisfied or frustrated. Similarly, if you have a perceptual experience, the content of the experience has to determine when it is good or bad. I am suggesting that it gets its content because the conditions of it being a good case are built into the causal structure of the experience. Red just is the feature that causes these sorts of experiences. Of course we can characterize that so that it sounds trivial: the experience is one of looking to be red. But the point is that there is a way of characterizing that experience which explains why it is a case of seeming to see something red. So we explain why it has the intentionality it does, even though it is an event in the world like any other. We start with the fact that the conscious perceptual experience has presentational intentionality built into it. And we can explain the actual content of the intentionality in terms of the causal component in the experience itself and its relation to the object in the world.

I resume discussion of this issue, with regard to the Brain in a Vat thought experiment, in the next chapter.

XII. SUMMARY OF THE RESULTS SO FAR

I am trying to get a nontrivial characterization of the raw phenomenology of the visual experience which will entail that it has a specific condition of satisfaction. The first principle is that every conscious perceptual experience is experienced as caused and caused by the object perceived. But that does not yet give us the specificity we want, because anything can cause anything. The specificity comes in when we note that for a class of features, being that feature is partly constituted by being able to cause that perceptual experience. Being red just is the ability to cause experiences of type Glog. That is where you get the internal connection between the type of experience and the type of object perceived. This is how the qualitative character of the subjective visual field presents the features of the objective visual field. For the basic features, here is how it works.

We assume, first, that the organism is conscious. Second, we suppose that in its field of consciousness there are some forms that are intrinsically intentional. Specifically, we assume that there is a specific form of visual and tactile intentionality. Given these assumptions, we need four steps:

1. Perception is hierarchical. All complex perception bottom out in basic perceptions of basic features. We are trying to explain the perception of basic features.
2. The perceptual experiences have specific intrinsic intentionality. There is no way I can have this experience without it seeming to me that I am seeing an F.
3. The subjective visual field contains intentional causation. There is no way I can have this experience without it seeming to me that it is caused by the feature I am seeing. I am seeing the object with its features that cause the experience. This is the fundamental Background presupposition.
4. The way the experience gets F as its condition of satisfaction is that F consists (at least in part) in the ability to cause experiences like this. This is the internal connection between the content F and the F state of affairs perceived. The form of causation

is intentional causation: the cause produces a conscious intentional perceptual content that presents the cause as the object of the perception.

5. This is why there is an internal and necessary connection between the character of the experience and the feature perceived. The object of the experience is its cause and these features are defined by their ability, it is their essential character, to cause these sorts of experiences.

We have now at least a tentative solution for our problem concerning the basic perceptual features. But this solution opens more questions than it answers. How about higher level features? How, for example, does the fact that it is a car get presented by the raw phenomenology? Furthermore, so far I have discussed only general features like "being red," but what about specific features like "being *my car*"? And what about all the traditional worries of spectrum inversion, color and size constancy, the inferential features of perception? And what about the famous "Brain in a Vat" problem? If I am a brain in a vat, the perceptual content can be exactly the same even though it is never veridical. We will take up these issues and others in the next chapter.

Chapter 5

How Perceptual Intentionality Works, Part Two

Extending the Analysis to Non-basic Features

The question we are attempting to answer is not at all simple. It is: how does the raw phenomenology intrinsically carry the conditions of satisfaction that it does? Another formulation is: how does the character of the perceptual experience determine the content that it does? A requirement of the answer is that the connection must be necessary or internal. It could not be that very experience if it did not have those conditions of satisfaction. So the metaphor of "raw" in our initial formulation can be misleading because the experience is not raw, it is loaded with intentionality. The experience must have features that determine the specific intentionality that it has and yet it must be possible to characterize those features in a non-intentionalist vocabulary. Why? Because the perceptual experience is just a raw piece of brute phenomenological data and we must characterize the phenomenology in a way that shows how it determines the intentionality.

Previous attempts to answer this question that I am aware of fail, usually because they just identify two entities, the experience and its object, without showing why that experience has to have that object or that type of object as its condition of satisfaction. Resemblance and causation both fail for reasons I have stated in the previous chapter. Just identifying two similar phenomena as resembling each other (resemblance) or standing in a cause-and-effect relation (causation) does not make one an intentional presentation of the other. The answer I proposed for the basic features is that if the animal has conscious perceptual intentionality, then the existence of a conscious experience of qualitative type Q within its subjective visual field—*where Q is experienced as caused by its object*—will necessarily have the content "I am seeing an object of type F," where F is essentially the capacity to cause experiences of type Q.

As usual, the point can be seen in a simpler form if we consider touch. I run my hand along the top surface of my desk. The intentional content is that the surface is smooth. Why? There is a certain character to the experience and *being smooth* is, at least in part, the capacity to cause sensations that have this character. In ordinary English, we would say that the object is smooth because it feels smooth, and smooth for middle-sized objects like this *just is* the capacity to cause this sort of experience. But remember, "feels smooth" explains nothing. It is like "looks red." But we explain what it means for something to "look red" or "feel smooth" in terms of its capacity to cause certain sorts of experiences.

As should be expected, the parallel between action and perception holds perfectly. Perceptual experiences have the mind-to-world direction of fit and the world-to-mind direction of causation. Intentions-in-action (experiences of acting) have the world-to-mind direction of fit and the mind-to-world direction of causation. For basic actions and basic perceptions the intentional content is internally related to the conditions of satisfaction, even though it is characterized non-intentionalistically, because being the feature F perceived consists in the ability to cause experiences of that type. And in the case of action, experiences of that type consists in their ability to cause that sort of bodily movement.

And remember we are talking about intentional causation throughout. There is plenty of other billiard-ball causation going on at different levels of the physiology and neurophysiology. But in the case of presentational intentional causation, the visual experience is experienced as caused by its object and the intention-in-action is experienced as causing the bodily movement.

I. FROM BOTTOM TO TOP OF VISUAL PERCEPTION

In this chapter we will extend the analysis beyond basic perceptual features. The bottom level of perception is in the perception of the basic features. What is the top level? Intuitively, we feel that I literally see that it is a California coastal redwood, but I do not literally see that he is drunk or that she is intelligent. What is the difference? Intuitively, what we are trying to determine is which features are *visible*. And intuitively, it seems to me the idea has to be that the visible features are those whose presence can be settled through vision. You may not be able to settle the presence of the features for sophisticated scientific purposes. But for practical purposes, you can settle the question of whether or not something is a California coastal redwood by its *appearance*. Of course, if it really mattered desperately we would want an examination of DNA. But for practical everyday purposes, being a California coastal redwood is a visible property of a class of trees. In a court of law, for example, a forest ranger could testify with certainty that the crime took place under a California redwood tree because he could see the tree at the time he saw the crime.

This is the criterion I propose for the cut-off point of the top level in visual and other forms of perceptual intentionality. If it is the case that seeing that the object has the property F is a genuine report of a visual experience, then property F must be a visible property. And if it is a visible property, for practical purposes, its presence can be ascertained by vision. You cannot settle whether or not somebody is intelligent or drunk just by looking at them (though you might get certain clues), but you can settle whether or not that tree over there is a California coastal redwood by its appearance. Again, this is for practical purposes, not theoretical scientific ones. This criterion is somewhat vague, but I think the vagueness probably mirrors the vagueness in our ordinary conception of the visual.

It might seem as if the criterion for basicness is dramatically different from the criterion for the top level. Basicness is settled by the brute facts of our physiology. What can we perceive without perceiving anything else by way of perceiving it? But the top level is settled by our epistemology. How would you settle the question, "What is it really?" However, I think in fact these are consistent and the top level is a natural development of the basic level. In both cases, our concept of the visual is set by what we can find out by looking. You can find out by looking that the object is red, and you can find out by looking that another object is a California redwood tree. In both cases what you get by looking is a certain set of perceptual experiences caused by the object in question. These are some of the ideas I am going to explore in this chapter.

II. THREE-DIMENSIONAL PERCEPTIONS

What about the perception of depth? I can literally see from where I sit that the couch is further from me than the chair. There is no question about the intentionality of the visual experience that it fixes the three-dimensional spatial relations. How does that work?

Here is a hypothesis I want to explore. I will state it crudely and then modify it more carefully in a moment. Crudely, the subjective visual field is, so to speak, two-dimensional. But that cannot be a correct thing to say, because that is the Bad Argument. The subjective visual field is not a visible object having two dimensions. But what

I mean by that is this: whatever you get in the subjective visual field by way of depth you can get from a two-dimensional stimulus. So, leaving out stereopsis for the moment, any impression of depth can be created by two-dimensional surfaces, as is shown by, for example, trompe-l'oeil paintings. We can ignore stereopsis because the perception of depth can be had with just one eye open. One-eyed vision is not as accurate as having both eyes, but what we are trying to explain is how you get from the basic perceptual features to the perception of depth so that the two-dimensional object is configured in such a way that it looks exactly like a three-dimensional object even to one eye. What does the object, whether two- or three-dimensional, produce in the subjective visual field? What it produces are the basic visual experiences, the subjective visual correlates of colors, lines, angles, textures, shapes, etc. The hypothesis I now want to explore is that the principles of perspective that so revolutionized Western painting are themselves part of the Background capacity of any competent perceiver in such a way that the perceiver is able to see the world as having three dimensions because of his Background mastery of perspective. So, for example, as you walk along, the experiences of objects that are getting closer occupy a bigger portion of the subjective visual field and the experiences of those retreating behind you, if you look back, are occupying a smaller portion of the subjective visual field. All the same, you have "size constancy." If asked, did the objects look as if they changed size? The answer is no, they looked the same size. But you are able to see the world as you see it because of the cognitive capacity to interpret the experiential content in a certain way. (More about size constancy in Section V.)

The function of the so-called laws of perspective can now be stated more precisely. The visual system has nothing to go on except the impact of light on the retina, together with such Background dispositional capacities and Network intentional states as the agent may possess. The impact of the light on the visual system will produce effects in the subjective visual field that are consequences of the laws of perspective. So, if you are looking at the railroad tracks extending away from you into the distance, your subjective visual field will contain the subjective correlates of two lines getting progressively closer together toward the top of the objective visual field. The basic subjective elements do not fix the conditions of satisfaction of three-dimensional space by themselves. But given our Background mastery of perspective, the subjective visual field carries an intentional content that has the three-dimensional as its conditions of satisfaction. The subjective visual field carries the intentional content: I am seeing railroad tracks receding in the distance. I am not saying that the entities in the subjective visual field present railroad tracks because they look like railroad tracks. They do not look like anything, because they are not and cannot be seen. Rather, because of their features and given my Background mastery of perspective, what I am seeing in the objective visual field looks like railroad tracks.

The witness said, "I saw an object that was a perfect cube." But of course, the basic visual experience was not of a cube. The basic perceptual features consisted of a set of connecting and crossing lines. Given the subject's mastery of perspective, these lines are perceived as a cube.

The upshot of this discussion is the following: Depth is not a basic perceptual feature. The basic visual experiences are of color, lines, angles, shapes, etc., but depth is perceived as a non-basic feature of the objective visual field because of the Background mastery of the principles of perspective.

There are several important points here about painting and its history. Gombrich points out that with the increased understanding of the principles of perspective, painters can now easily achieve feats that were inconceivable to Medieval painters. As Gombrich says, "[M]any a modest amateur has mastered tricks that would have looked like sheer magic to Giotto. Perhaps even the crude colored renderings we find on a box of breakfast cereal would have made Giotto's contemporaries gasp."[1] Prior to the Renaissance, painters typically tried to reproduce the geometry of the object itself and not to produce an image on a canvas that would cause in us an experience that would be like looking at the object. Because they understood perspective, Renaissance and post-Renaissance artists were able to produce visual representations that would have effects on the viewer similar to those of the actual object itself, and they did this by producing in the viewer an experience that had basic perceptual features that would give the impression of seeing something like the object itself, given the perspectival situation of the perception. The Impressionists went a step further and, according to some accounts, tried to draw the impression itself. If the account that I am giving is correct, that is not a well-defined enterprise because the impression is not something that can be seen.

We have to be extremely careful how we relate the characteristic of the experience to the characteristics of its conditions of satisfaction. It is commonly said (or at least it was in my intellectual childhood) that the reason El Greco painted such elongated figures is that he actually had an eye defect that made everything look elongated to him. On this theory, when El Greco saw a person who would look ordinary to us, the person looked elongated to El Greco, and so he painted an elongated person. If you reflect on this, it makes no sense. Suppose that it were true, that an ordinary person who looks normal to me looked elongated to El Greco. If El Greco painted exactly what he saw, he would have painted a person who looks ordinary to me and consequently elongated to him. But if he painted a person who looks elongated to me, then his own painting of that person would look hyper-elongated to him because the hypothesis is that people who

1. Gombrich, E. H. *Art and Illusion: A Study in the Psychology of Pictorial Representation.* Princeton, NJ: Princeton University Press, 1960, 8.

look ordinary to me already look elongated to him. The hypothesis, in short, that he painted distorted figures because a normal stimulus looks distorted to him makes no sense, because if he is reproducing on the canvas what produces distortions in him, then he will simply reproduce what looks normal to the rest of us.

III. TEMPORAL RELATIONS

What about Time? We have so far analyzed how the non-intentional features of subjective visual experiences can give them intrinsic intentionality for colors, lines, shapes, and space. What about temporal relations? Temporal relations are *literally* part of the subjective field. So I saw the red ball before I saw the green cube and before that, I saw the blue triangle. The temporality of the three relations is literally a feature of the subjective visual field. I had this experience before that experience and that experience before that other experience. It is easy enough to induce perceptual illusions about time because the time of the experience does not match perfectly the experience of time. But all the same, the subjective experience of temporal relations does in fact have features that set conditions of satisfaction. It is important to emphasize that they do this not because of the matching relation, but because of a combination of the causal relations and consciousness. The sequence of objective events A, B, and C causes in me subjective experiences of A, followed by B, followed by C.

The capacity to cause in me conscious experiences that are temporally related in a certain way automatically gives the sequence of experiences the intentional content that their objects are related temporally. Why? Does this not violate our principle that resemblance is not enough for intentionality? No. What I am arguing is that the sequence in the subjective visual field is experienced as a presentation of a sequence in the objective visual field, precisely for the same reason as the earlier cases: for the events in the objective field to be related in that way is precisely for them to be able to cause experiences that have these relations.

IV. EXTENDING THE ANALYSIS UPWARD

I have so far explained how the raw phenomenology of perceptual experience sets basic features of the world as conditions of satisfaction, and I have extended the analysis to consider the perception of depth and other spatial relations. We now have to consider higher-level features. For example, what fact about this perception makes it a perception of *a certain type of tree* and what fact about this perception makes it a perception of *my car*?

In my garden there is a tree that I recognize as a California coastal redwood. I have no difficulty in recognizing a California coastal redwood from a giant sequoia, or for that matter California live-oaks or eucalyptus trees. Tree identification, by the way, is rather easy in California because there are so few native species, whereas in a state like Vermont there are a large number of native species.

The ordinary language notions of "looks" and "looks like" rely heavily on the notion of resemblance. So if I say "it looks like a redwood tree," then I seem to be saying it resembles other redwood trees. The hypothesis I want to explore now is that something's being a redwood tree involves how it looks and involves its visual features, and these are not resemblance relations but these are, so to speak, independently specifiable features. I learned to identify redwood trees by actually seeing redwood trees. The result is that when I see a redwood tree I see it *as a redwood tree*, and I see that it *is a redwood tree*. Both the "seeing as" and "seeing that" part are contained in this, but this higher-level feature is based on the identification of the basic features—the colors and shapes, etc.—as being those of a redwood tree.

In the case of the basic features, the hypothesis we explored was that there is a conceptual or necessary connection between the feature and the corresponding perceptual experience because the feature is in part defined as the ability to cause that sort of perceptual experience, and the experience is had as caused by its object. So the relation of intentional presentation is necessary and not conventional. There is no way I can have the experience of red without it seeming to me that I am seeing something red, because red is in part defined as the ability to cause that sort of experience. The situation is much more complicated for a redwood tree, but the same or similar principles apply. Being a redwood tree is in part constituted by having the visible features of a redwood tree and having those features is a matter of causing certain sorts of visual experiences. But looking like a redwood tree is a matter of causing certain sorts of visual experiences, so the capacity to cause visual experiences is shared by both the color red and California coastal redwoods. And in both cases it can seem to me that I am seeing something red or seeing a California coastal redwood for essentially the same reason; that is, having the visual features of a redwood is in part constituted by being able to cause experiences like this.

The simplest sorts of upward non-basic perceptual features would be those that are, so to speak, additive; that those are arrived at by simply adding the components that constitute the basic features. And I think we can do something like that with species of trees. I have learned to recognize a certain sort of tree as a California coastal redwood. In virtue of *what* do I so recognize it? I recognize it in virtue of the fact that there is a particular set of features to the structure of the tree and the structure of fronds that constitute the visible features of the California redwood. Now the features that go to make up the fronds' colors and shapes, and the bark color, shape, and texture, are all basic features. I can make a composite of the basic features to get the totality. I have been taught that anything that causes this sort of visual experience is a California coastal redwood. For such a case, we simply extend the analysis of the basic features to entities that are compositional functions of the basic features. Of course, for scientific or legal or other technical purposes we would want a genetic examination of the DNA to see whether or not something really was a California redwood. All the same, for practical and other purposes visual experience is sufficient. If it has all of the perceptible features of a California redwood, then for practical purposes it is identifiable as a California redwood.

The compositional character of many high level features can be quite complex, and yet still produce distinct perceptual experiences. Think of wine tasting. Wine tasters are typically taught to discriminate various basic components of the taste of wine, such as alcohol, residual grape sugar, tannin, acetic acid, etc. They then learn to tell a difference between a Cabernet Sauvignon and a Pinot Noir, and they are taught along the model that I have been describing. A Cabernet Sauvignon is a wine that typically causes *this sort* of gustatory and olfactory experiences, and a Pinot Noir is one that causes *this sort* of gustatory and olfactory experiences. Notice that I am not making the mistake of the traditional psychological atomists who attempted to build complex ideas out of simple ideas. But many higher-level features are combinations of lower-level features. In the case of wine, tasting of the lower-level features tends to be transformed by the total blend.

V. RECOGNITION AND THE PROBLEM OF PARTICULARITY

So far we have considered only the perception of instances of general properties, such as red or being a California coastal redwood. I now turn to the problem of perceiving particular objects.

In *Intentionality* (1983),[2] I pointed out there is a special problem of how the conditions of satisfaction pick up a *particular* object, rather than an object of a certain type. From Bill Jones's point of view, there has to be a difference from the experience when he takes to be seeing a woman who looks exactly like his wife Sally Jones and when he takes himself to be seeing Sally herself. I said that the way to answer that problem is to specify in the conditions of satisfaction not just that a woman with particular Sally-like features is before Bill and that her presence and features are causing Bill's visual experience, but that she is identical with the woman that Bill has seen on countless previous occasions. So you get an identity relation between the object perceived and objects that are referred to by other elements of the Network and the Background. At any rate, that was the solution I proposed to this problem in 1983. The problem I did not address then but want to address now is, how does all this get to be part of the phenomenology? What fact about the subjective visual experience makes it the case that it is satisfied only by a particular object rather than by an object of a certain type? Even though the subject may be deceived on particular occasions by the fact that the two objects are indiscriminable, all the same, there has to be something about his phenomenology that makes it the case that only one of the objects that satisfy the general conditions will be the one that satisfies his particular visual experience. In common-sense terms, the question here is about *recognition*. The point is not just that one has an experience of seeing a particular car or a particular person, but that one *recognizes* that car as his car and he *recognizes* that person as his spouse. I suggested that a formal way to put recognition into the conditions of satisfaction is simply to point out that there are previous experiences that the perceiver has had of a particular object, and that

2. Searle, John R. *Intentionality: An Essay in the Philosophy of Mind.* Cambridge: Cambridge University Press, 1983.

the object he is now seeing is identical with the object that caused those previous experiences. The solution that I proposed in 1983 for the Network is, using my 1983 notation, given as follows:

We are supposing that Jones has an experience whose form is

1. Vis exp (Sally is there and her presence and features are causing this visual experience)

as distinct from

2. Vis exp (a woman with identical Sally-like features is there and her presence and features are causing this visual experience).

The relation of the Network to the present intentional content from Jones's point of view is

3. I have had in the past a set of experiences $x, y, z, \ldots$ caused by the presence and features of a woman whom I have known as Sally and I have at present a set of memories of these experiences $a, b, c, \ldots$ which are such that my present visual experience is:

Vis exp (a woman with identical Sally-like features is before me and her presence and features are causing this visual experience, and that woman is identical with the woman whose presence and features caused $x, y, z, \ldots$ which in turn caused $a, b, c, \ldots$)

I think this analysis is correct as far as the conditions of satisfaction are concerned. To repeat the question, how do those conditions of satisfaction get to be realized in the phenomenology? What fact about the experience, construed as a raw piece of phenomenology, carries those conditions of satisfaction? The question is made more pressing by the fact that since Wittgenstein, we have become extremely suspicious of the idea that there might be some special experience of recognizing. But ordinary language is a good clue that there are some features to the phenomenology. So we say things like, not just that it looks like such and such a type of car, it *looks like my car*. Imagine that a man is married to one of two identical twins who are so identical that on purely visual grounds he cannot discriminate one from another. All the same, if he thinks he is seeing his wife, she will look different. Why? Because she looks like *my wife*. This is the phenomenology we now need to explore. Furthermore, as with my car, my office, my family, etc., *it looks familiar*. And what is the phenomenology of looking familiar? As usual, illusions are philosophically important. A common visual illusion is *déjà vu*. The phenomenology of déjà vu is that you see a scene that you have good reasons to suppose you have never seen before, but all the same, it looks familiar. It is something that has already been seen, something that is déjà vu.

The way that we have been exploring the phenomenology is by a combination of causation and consciousness. You have conscious forms of intentionality where intentional causation gives you an experience. The features of the experience that enable it to present this type of object are defined in terms of the ability of this type of object to cause this type of experience, where that ability is part of the essence of what it is to be that type of object. How do we get the notion of recognition of a particular object into that account of the phenomenology? I do not know for sure, but here is how I think it works. In the case of recognition, I do not just have the experience as caused by an object that has a *general* feature such as red, but I have an experience with a particular character which is experienced as caused by *repeated occurrences* of the same particular object. Or, strictly speaking, *repeated occurrences of experiences caused by that object*. From an intentionality point of view, the reason my car looks familiar is that I have seen it nearly every day for the past ten years. When I see it, I do not just see *a car*; rather, the particular phenomenology of my experience is that the experience is caused by an object that has caused other repeated experiences of this type. It is the repetition in the phenomenology that enables it to nail down recognition of the particular. The character of this experience is not just that it is caused by seeing a car; rather, it is caused by seeing a car where that very car has in the past caused other such visual experiences. In other words, the visual experience is not just the terminal point in a sequence of visual experience, but it is *experienced as* the latest in a sequence of such visual experiences. And this I think is the essence of "looking familiar," which gives us the phenomenology of recognition.

Notice, as usual, that there is nothing self-guaranteeing about the phenomenology. I can have the phenomenology of it looking to be my car when it is not in fact my car, but the phenomenology is different when I see it as my car from when I just see it as looking a lot like my car. What I am trying to get at is how the sequence of experiences generates the phenomenology of recognition.

To put the statement of the phenomenology in the simplest form, the experience of seeing that it is *my car*, as opposed to the experience of seeing that it is a car with such-and-such features, are at least in part:

> I am having a visual experience caused by a car with such-and-such features and this visual experience is latest in a sequence of visual experiences caused by that very car. Furthermore, I know independently that the car that caused the sequence of experiences is my car.

Notice certain things about this analysis. The first is that I am trying to get recognition as having to do with the identity of the cause of a sequence of experiences, but the ownership relation is not itself a visual property. That is why I have to put it as something independent of the phenomenology. You can see this in the case of a mistake. If it was not in fact the same car as the one I saw before, then I made an error in my perceptual judgment. But if it turned out I had never owned a car, that there was a flaw in the ownership documents, then there need be nothing at all wrong with my *perceptual* judgment.

I was mistaken about a fact that exists independently of perceptual phenomenology.

VI. SOLUTION OF SOME OUTSTANDING QUESTIONS ABOUT PERCEPTION

There are a series of questions that we have left unanswered and I now intend to address them directly.

Question 1: Does all perception of material objects require inferences?

Can I see a whole tree or do I have to infer the presence of the whole tree from just seeing one side? It seems that I must be inferring, and yet phenomenologically the experience is one of seeing a whole tree. It is just phenomenologically wrong to say I inferred something.

I believe the notion of a basic perceptual property resolves this puzzle. The basic properties are such things as the size, shape, color, and texture of what is presented to me. In order to see the whole tree, I have to see the basic perceptual properties that are presented to me. Whether or not we should think of the perception of the whole object as involving an inference depends on how we define "inference." If we mean that there has to be a conscious act of inferring, then there is typically no such conscious act. It is almost always false to say that I *infer* that there is a whole tree there. If we define "inference" so that an inference occurs when the informational content of the whole subjective visual experience is larger than the informational content of the perception of the basic properties, then there is an inference. The important point for the present discussion is that *being a tree* is not a basic perceptual feature. The basic perceptual features in this case are colors, shapes, textures, etc. Even depth, as we have seen, is not a basic perceptual feature, and this is shown by the fact of seeing the three-dimensional aspect of the tree can be produced by the perception of a two-dimensional surface.

Question 2: How does the account deal with color constancy and size constancy?

I will consider these in order. Imagine that a shadow falls over a portion of the red ball so that part of it is in shadow and part not. Did the part in shadow change its color? Well, obviously not, and it is obviously not *seen as* having changed its color. All the same, there is a difference in the subjective visual field. The subjective basic perceptual properties have changed. The proof is that if I were drawing a picture of what I now see, I would have to include a darker portion of the part in shadow, even though I know that there has been no change in its actual color. It is extremely misleading to describe this phenomenon as "color constancy," because of course the experienced color is precisely not constant. It is because of my higher-level Background capacities that I am able to see it as having the same color even though at the lower level I see it as having in part changed its color. I want to emphasize this point. At the basic level, there is no such thing as color constancy. At the basic level, the color is precisely not constant, neither subjectively nor objectively. It changes. It is just at the higher level that I know, because of my Background abilities, that it still keeps the same color.

Now let us apply these lessons to the problem of size constancy. I see a row of trees in front of me. They all look the same size, even though at the basic level the trees farther away look smaller because of the difference of the impact of the distant trees and the nearby trees on my subjective visual field. As I walk along the row of trees, the subjective visual field changes to accommodate this change in the perspective. My intentional content at the higher level is that the trees are always the same size, but at the lower level there is no question that there is a change in the basic perceptual properties.

The upshot of this discussion of color and size constancy is that at the basic level neither exists. At the basic level color and size change, and at a higher level, because of our (presumably genetically encoded) Background mastery of perceptual abilities, we see objects in changing light conditions and in changing distances away from us as having the same color and the same size.

Question 3: What about the traditional problem of spectrum inversion?

We imagine a population consisting of two sections of people, each section enjoying a different experience of red and green from the other section. Thus, if I am a member of one section, what I call "seeing red" will be such that if the members of the other section had that experience, they would call it "seeing green." None of this comes out in behavior because the behavior is the same for both sections of the population. They both start when the traffic light turns green and stop when it turns red.

I will argue that though their behavior is the same, their perceptions have different intentional contents. I am not suggesting that this is an unproblematic thought experiment. It may be neurobiologically impossible.[3] But we are doing a philosophical thought experiment and not engaging in speculative neurophysiology, so neurophysiological possibility and impossibility are irrelevant. So let us assume that the thought experiment is O.K. Now then, if you ask yourself the question, "what fact about this experience makes it the case that it is an experience whose conditions of satisfaction are that there is a green object there?", there is a puzzle because by hypothesis, in the red and green inversion case, the two sections of the population identify exactly the same objects as red and the same objects as green, even though the experiences that they have are different and mutually exclusive. To make the question even

---

3. Palmer, Stephen E. *Vision Science: Photons to Phenomenology*. Cambridge, MA: MIT Press, 1999.

sharper, imagine that I could shift from being a member of one section of the population to being a member of another at will, that I have a switch attached to my head that enables me to switch over from red experience to green experience and from green experience to red experience, even though the stimulus is constant. When I am driving, I will have to remember which state I am in, otherwise what looks like a green light will in fact be a red light, and conversely. I know that the light that now looks a color I now call "red," ten minutes ago I would have called "green." Now I call it "red" because I am in the red/green stage, not the green/red stage. The question becomes sharper because it can no longer be answered by saying, "it is the essence of this qualitative experience that it is satisfied by red things and not satisfied by green things." This is because in the case we have imagined, the same person with the same qualitative experience can have that experience satisfied by either a red thing or a green thing, depending on which state he is in.

The question is, do the sections have the same or different intentional contents? Let me block one answer to this question before it even gets started, the answer that says that the question does not make any sense. We would have to be supposing that "green" and "red" are words of a private language if we thought that there was any difference between the two cases. If the population identifies the same objects as red and the same objects as green, then it is strictly meaningless to suppose that they have different experiences on the inside. Here is a simple illustration that this answer will not do. Consider Monet's painting of the field of poppies, reproduced as plate 5 in the color plates section following page 74. Now go through a red and green inversion in your mind, make all the red poppies look green and the green grass look red. It is a different picture altogether and the experience is different. The aesthetic experience is totally ruined. To demonstrate, I present the Monet, so altered, as plate 6 along with the original:[4]

---

4. I am indebted to Matt Langione for this illustration.

If, as I have been claiming, it is a matter of some importance that other people share visual experiences with me, then how am I so confident that they do not in fact have spectrum inversion? How am I so confident that we are both having the same sort of experience when we look at the Monet? The answer, I think, is obvious. We have similar visual machinery in our heads. If you take cases where we are confident that organisms do not have similar visual experiences, you can see the basis for the difference. It is commonly said in neurobiology textbooks that cats have different color vision from humans. Now, philosophically speaking, that looks like a stunning claim. How could the scientists possibly know what it is like to have cats' visual experiences? And the answer is that they can look at the difference between the cats' color receptors and our color receptors. They can be completely confident in making judgments about the cats' experience based on the knowledge of the neurobiological basis of the experience, and this is why I can be completely confident that other people do not suffer from spectrum inversion. If they did, they would have to have a different perceptual apparatus for color vision, and the available evidence is that, pathologies apart, there is a commonality in human color perception.

It is a Background presupposition of our use of color vocabulary that there is a commonality to different people's perceptions of red, green, blue, etc. The basis for making this Background presupposition, if it were challenged, is that we know that the mechanisms that produce these experiences are relevantly the same in different people. This, by the way, is how we define normal vision. If you do not share these capacities, you have, in one way or another, defective vision. As a thought experiment, we can imagine cases where we are systematically mistaken about how other people perceive colors because they have a spectrum inversion which is not detectable by standard behavioral tests. All the same, in these cases we would be able to detect that they had different color experiences if we had a full knowledge of their perceptual physiology. If there were such people, it would turn out that they do not mean by "red" and "green" what the rest of us mean by red and green. There is a systematic failure of communication. As a thought experiment, this is possible; as a neurobiological hypothesis, I think it is out of the question. Red objects are those which cause color experiences *like this one* and green objects are objects which cause color experiences *like that one*. If there really were spectrum-inverted people, it would turn out that they mean something different by these words and their meaning something different has to be detected by neurobiological tests and not by the usual behavioral tests.

VII. THE BRAIN IN THE VAT

A related but even more radical thought experiment in philosophy is to imagine that one might be a brain in a vat (I began the discussion of this in Chapter 2). I used to use this thought experiment fairly often, but it was so frequently misunderstood that I have more or less stopped using it. (A standard misunderstanding was to suppose I was raising the skeptical problem, how do know I am not a brain in a vat?) However, the thought experiment raises interesting issues for this book, so I am going to resume discussion of it.

The basic idea of the thought experiment is that while I am fully aware that I am living in the twenty-first century in California, the sheer phenomenology of my experience is consistent with the possibility that I might, for example, be a brain in a vat of nutrients in a laboratory in Duluth, Minnesota, in the twenty-fifth century. Stimuli are being fed into my brain through an elaborate computer system using a tape of previously occurring experiences. Fortunately for me, I was given a twentieth- and twenty-first-century tape so that my experiences would be just like those of someone who lived in California in the twentieth and the twenty-first centuries. The computer stimulates the brain directly without going through the sense organs. The whole point of the thought experiment rests on the presumably true assumptions that brain processes are sufficient to produce phenomenology, and that the cranium is a kind of a vat. In an important sense, we are in fact brains in vats, because the actual brain is situated in the vat of my cranium. The real difference between real life and the brain in the vat fantasy is that my real-life vat is attached to the rest of my body and the stimuli going to my brain come from features of the real world stimulating my peripheral nerve endings through perception and other parts of my nervous system. Also in real life, free will is at least a possibility. But for the brain in the vat, all its experiences, including those of "free action," are determined. The whole point of the thought experiment is that my subjective qualitative experiences, my phenomenology, could be exactly the same even though I was radically disconnected from the world.

There are several things to notice about the thought experiment. First, it is resolutely first-personal. The fantasy is not that he, she, or you might be a brain in a vat. I can obviously see that he, she, or you are not in a vat. The whole point is that my experience of apparently seeing that other people are not brains in vats, and all my other experiences, are consistent with the possibility that I still might be a brain in a vat. The thought is not that somebody somewhere might be a brain in a vat, but that I, right here and now, with these very experiences, could still be a brain in a vat. The thought experiment is first-personal, but like Descartes's *cogito*, it is a variable first-person pronoun. "I think, therefore I exist" does not mean René Descartes thinks, therefore he exists, but that any person at all can have the thought "I think, therefore I exist."

The second point is that the thought experiment makes sense only on the assumption that the phenomenology is exactly the same in the two cases. What would my life be like if I were such a brain in a vat? As far as my conscious experiences are concerned, it would be exactly the same as it is now. Exactly the same.

Third, the point of the thought experiment is not necessarily epistemic. You could use it as an entry in the skepticism of, "how do I know that I am not (just) a brain in a vat?" But that does not seem to me an interesting aspect of the thought experiment. I am more interested in the way that we can separate the ontologically subjective character of experience from the ontologically objective features of the real world that experience gives us access to.

Fourth, there is nothing Cartesian in the thought experiment; it does not imply that the mental and the physical are in two different ontological realms. It just asserts that it is possible for us to have the qualitative, ontologically subjective, biologically given conscious experiences, which are "physical" phenomena like any other biological phenomena, without the experiences being connected in the right way to the real world. The postulation of the brain in a vat as a thought experiment does not imply Cartesianism in any form.

If I were a brain in a vat, most of my beliefs would be false. Almost all of my perceptual beliefs would be false. So I now believe that I see a desk in front of me and hear traffic noise from outside. In the fantasy case, both of those beliefs would be false. The interesting question is how much of the intentional *content* of my consciousness would remain if the phenomenology were the same but the causal connection to the world was radically altered. In an extreme version of the causal externalist theory of meaning—the view that says that the intentional content of my beliefs and the meanings of my words are entirely fixed by their causes—if I were a brain in a vat, I would have to believe that I was a brain in a vat. This is because the fact that I am a brain in a vat is causing whatever it is that I think and say. This view was advanced by both Davidson[5] and Putnam.[6] It follows from their version of externalism that the content of my belief is fixed by its causes. According to Davidson, it is thus necessarily the case that most of my beliefs are true. If I am a brain in a vat, I must believe that I am a brain in a vat and that belief is true. On this view, when I say to myself right now, "I believe I live in Berkeley, California, in the twenty-first century," what I really mean and what I have to mean is "I believe I am a brain in a vat in the twenty-fifth century." This result, I think, is a *reductio ad absurdum* of their versions of externalism. Remember, the whole thing is resolutely first-personal. I now say and believe that I live in Berkeley, California, in the second decade of the twenty-first century. In the fantasy, the cause of my saying that and pretty much the cause of my saying anything is that I am a brain in a vat in the twenty-fifth century being fed an artificial tape. So, on this version held by both Putnam and Davidson, though I say the words "I believe I live in Berkeley, California, etc.," what those words actually mean, and what the content of my belief is, is that I am a brain in a vat in Duluth, Minnesota, in the twenty-fifth century. Remember, we are talking about me right here and now, on the hypothesis that, unknown to me, I am a brain in a vat of the sort described, and it turns out on the externalist view that the content of my belief is radically different from what I take it to be. This view is so counterintuitive that it is hard to take it seriously. I will not work out more of its absurdities because it is not relevant to my main concern, which is about the content of perception.

But if causal externalism is wrong about the determination of intentional content, then how does my account of the determination of

5. Davidson, Donald, reported in McDowell, John, *Mind and World*. Cambridge, MA: Harvard University Press, 1996, 16–17.

6. Putnam, Hilary. *Reason, Truth and History*. Cambridge: Cambridge University Press, 1981, 14–15.

perceptual intentional content fit with the brain-in-the-vat fantasy? If in large part the phenomenology determines intentional content, and if the phenomenology is the same in the two cases, then I seem to be committed to the view that the intentional content is pretty much the same for the brain in the vat as it is for me even though nearly all of my beliefs are false in the brain-in-a-vat case.

I think in fact that is the right result. If I am right now a brain in a vat, all the same I believe that I am a philosopher living in Berkeley, California, in the early decades of the twenty-first century. The whole point of the thought experiment is that the phenomenology in the brain-in-a-vat case is identical to the phenomenology in the veridical case. And to the extent that the phenomenology fixes intentional content, intentional content is identical. But there is a problem for me because of my claim that there is a "backward road" from object to intentional content. If red is what normally causes this visual experience, then why am I not literally seeing the cause of this experience, whatever it is, in the brain-in-a-vat case? How can I claim I am not seeing anything when it looks like my account of intentional content says that I am seeing the cause of my experience of red, even though I claim that in the brain-in-a-vat case I am not seeing anything? Suppose that in the brain-in-a-vat case, my experiences of red are systematically caused by electrical stimulus ESR (short for "Electrical Stimulus Red") and my experiences of a straight line are systematically caused by ESSL (short for "Electrical Stimulus Straight Line"). Why am I not perceiving ESR and ESSL? In order to answer this question, we have to make it clear that the account of causation I use in the explanation of perceptual intentional content is intentional causation throughout. In the veridical case, the object of perception is not just any old cause, but the object which is presented to me in the perceptual experience. But in the brain-in-a-vat case, the causation is not intentional causation. The causation is just like the neurobiological causation, which is essential to any perceptual experience but which is not itself the object of the experience. In the case of intentional causation, perceptual experience must be experienced as caused by its objects and the intentional content occurs as part of a Network of intentional contents and against the Background of capacities. So when I see red, I see it as a color and I see it as distinct from other colors such as blue and green. Furthermore, I see all of these as parts of an independently existing reality, a reality that exists entirely independent of my perception of it and independent of my body. In the brain-in-a-vat scenario, the phenomenology is the same but there is no object that satisfies the intentional content fixed by that phenomenology.

In the brain-in-a-vat fantasy, it is indeed as if I were experiencing red objects as causing my perceptual experience. But in the fantasy, there is no object there and the whole thing is a hallucination. What would it be like if I really did have perceptual beliefs about the vat in the brain-in-a-vat fantasy? Well, suppose the whole thing is rigged up so that the walls of the vat stimulate a perceptual experience in me as if I were seeing the walls of the vat. That would genuinely be a case of seeing the wall of the vat, and I would come to believe that I am seeing the wall of the vat. I am not sure about this, but I think the brain-in-a-vat fantasy can be accommodated within the account of the fixation of intentional content that I have provided. In the brain in a vat, when I think I see something red the conditions of satisfactions are still that I see something red. And that is because I take myself to be seeing something whose essence is to cause this sort of perceptional experience by intentional causation, but in fact I see nothing. So the difference between the good case and the bad case, between the case where I am really in Berkeley and the case where I am the brain in a vat, is that though the intentional content is the same, in one case it is satisfied and in the other it is not.

VIII. CONCLUSION

As I said earlier, this chapter and the preceding are the central theoretical chapters of the book. The question we are dealing with is how the raw phenomenology of the perceptual experience fixes the conditions of satisfaction that it does. In order that they should set the conditions of satisfaction (in the sense of requirement) that they do, there has to be an internal connection between the raw phenomenology and the actual features and states of affairs in the ontologically objective world that constitute the conditions of satisfaction (in the sense of things required). How can there be an internal connection, some sort of logical link, between what are obviously two independent sets of phenomena—raw feels on the one hand and real features of the real world on the other? The key to understanding this connection, the mediating term between the raw feel and the real features, is the presentational intentional causation of perceptual experience. Typically, philosophers in the past have been unable to see this because they did not understand the presentational intentionality of experience. And they did not see the extent to which perceptual experience is causal throughout and is experienced as causal throughout. Traditionally in analytic philosophy, discussions of causation suffer from an absurdly inadequate Humean conception. On this traditional view, causation is always a relation between discrete events instantiating a general law; and the causal relation, the "necessary connection," is never experienced. This view is inadequate. We live in a sea of consciously experienced causation. In every normal case of conscious perception and intentional action, the causal relation is experienced as part of the content and the conditions of satisfaction of the perceptual or intention-in-acting experiences. When you raise your arm, you experience your "trying" as causing your arm to go up. When you see your arm go up, you experience the movement of the arm as causing the visual experience that has the presence and features of the arm movement as the rest of its conditions of satisfaction. Far from it being the case that we never have an experience of causation, to repeat, we live in a *sea* of experienced causation. Every time you consciously perceive anything or do anything intentionally, you are experiencing causation.

If you understand something about presentational intentional causation, you can understand how the connection between perceptual experience and reality is mediated. In Chapter 4, I tried to show how at the most basic level, perceptual experiences are experienced as caused by their objects. And at the level of the basic perceptual features and basic perceptual experiences, the notion of something being F necessarily involves the notion of its causing certain sorts of experiences; and that is why those experiences have the condition of satisfaction of presenting something as F. That is, what it is to be an F is, in part, to cause those types of experiences.

In this chapter we extended that account to show:

1. How we could have three-dimensional perception on the basis of the basic experiences.
2. How we could have the perception of temporal relations.
3. How we could extend the analysis upward to deal with complex perceptions such as the perception of a redwood tree.
4. How we could deal with the problem of particularity.

The basic theme of these two chapters has been that there is an internal connection between the raw phenomenology of the perceptual experiences and the conditions of satisfaction set by those perceptual experiences.

Chapter 6

Disjunctivism

A Martian philosopher visiting Earth might be amazed at the amount of attention paid to hallucinations in philosophical discussions of perception and would not unreasonably conclude that hallucinations must be very common. In fact they are very rare. As far as I know, I have never had a hallucination in my life. The real-life cases one hears and reads about are typically either pathological or, more frequently, recreational. Schizophrenics commonly have auditory hallucinations where they "hear voices" and in some unusual ailments there are visual hallucinations. In the case of Pick's disease, the patient has visual hallucinations that are embedded in the real context, such that the patient might have a hallucination of a cat sitting on a real bookshelf in the real room. Recreational hallucinations were very common in the latter decades of the twentieth century, when many people took "hallucinogenic" drugs. I never did this, but I know people who did. But the sort of visual hallucinations that philosophers like to discuss with their "Brain in a Vat" and "evil demon" fantasies are very uncommon. All the same, the study of hallucinations is an important tool in philosophy, and would remain useful even if there had never been any actual hallucinations, for the following reason: in analyzing a conscious perception, it is crucial, as we have seen over and over, to be able to separate the ontologically subjective perceptual experience from the ontologically objective state of affairs perceived. Without making this distinction clearly we cannot account for the basic biology of perceptual experience which is the conscious intentionality in the brain of the perceiver and the causal relations between that intentionality and the state of affairs perceived. It is philosophically useful to us to discuss hallucinations because, by stipulation, the phenomenology of the hallucination and that of the veridical experience can be exactly the same.

And this is not just a fantasy. In the present situation, for example, I see the green table, but I could be having an experience type identical with this one and not be seeing anything. How is that possible? The cause of the visual experience begins with the reflection of photons in the objective visual field. After the stimulation of the photoreceptor cells, the internal processes in the nervous system are causally sufficient to produce the conscious visual experience. Once the visual stimulus is past the retina, the visual system knows nothing further about its external causes. How could it? So it is in principle possible to duplicate exactly the sequence of causal events minus the external stimulus. In fact, the conscious visual experience is fixed fairly far down the line in the visual system. According to Crick and Koch, V1 (Visual Area 1) has little, or possibly no, effect on the visual experience.[1] If you deny that the hallucinatory experience and the veridical experience—the bad case and the good case—can be phenomenologically and intentionalistically exactly the same, then you know you have made a mistake. If you have a theory that has that as a consequence, then you know the theory is false because it entails a false proposition. Amazingly, there is a class of philosophers of perception who accept precisely this *reductio ad absurdum*. They are called Disjunctivists.

1. Koch, Christof. *The Quest for Consciousness: A Neurobiological Approach*. Englewood, CO: Roberts & Co. Publishers, 2004, 105.

I think it ought to worry them that brain scientists who specialize in hallucination deny their view. Thus, in an article by ffytche et al.[2] reporting a study of hallucinations suffered by patients with Bonnet's syndrome, they report "the spontaneous visual percepts (visual hallucinations) experienced by these patients are identical to those associated with normal seeing, though they can be recognized because of their bizarre and often amusing character and because given the patients impaired vision, they are seen in greater detail then real stimuli." And in a separate popular article by ffytche, he reports that his response to the question, "What goes on in the brain when you hallucinate?" is "It's the same as when you experience real things."[3]

I. WHAT EXACTLY *IS* DISJUNCTIVISM?

There is now a huge literature on Disjunctivism, including some rather hefty secondary articles describing the field.[4] There are lots of different accounts and Disjunctivists do not agree amongst themselves exactly what the view is, but this is not surprising given that they are all philosophers. But a common feature that runs through Disjunctivism, and which I think can be used to define the notion, is that there is no common conscious experience that occurs in both the good and the bad cases. As Byrne and Logue say in the introduction to their collection of readings, "the experiences in the good case and the hallucinatory bad cases *share no mental core*, that is, there is *no (experiential)*

---

2. ffytche, D. H., R. J. Howard, David A. Brammer, P. Woodruff, and S. Williams. "The Anatomy of Conscious Vision: A fMRI Study of Visual Hallucinations." *Nature Neuroscience* (1998): 1, 738–42.

3. ffytche, D. H. "Hallucinations and the Cheating Brain." *World Science Festival* (2012).

4. Of these, the two I have found most useful are "Disjunctive Theory of Perception" by Matthew Soteriou in the *Stanford Encyclopedia of Philosophy* (http://plato.stanford.edu/entries/perception-disjunctive/) and "Disjunctivism" by William Fish in the Internet Encyclopedia of Philosophy (http://www.iep.utm.edu/disjunct/).

mental kind that characterizes both cases."[5] They go on to say there is
"no common element" [my italics throughout] to the experiences in
the good and the bad cases, where "good" means veridical and "bad"
means hallucinatory. The sense in which perception is then seen as
"disjunctive" is that there is supposed to be a disjunction between the
veridical and the hallucinatory cases.

But the fact that there is no general agreement on the definition of
Disjunctivism is actually a deep point and I will return to it. For the
moment, I will just leave the question blank and say that the thesis is
that there is no *blank* in common between the good and the bad
cases. Just to have some terminology to work with, I will define
Disjunctivism as the denial of the "commonality" thesis, where commonality implies that the *blank* is in common between the good and
bad cases.

It is important in what follows to emphasize that we are considering a fairly strict definition of Disjunctivism. For example, many
philosophers of perception who, like me, hold Direct Realist related
views are mistakenly called Disjunctivists. Barry Stroud is definitely
not a Disjunctivist, though I have heard him described as one. There
is a restricted class of people who are definitely Disjunctivists, and
the two best known to me are my colleagues John Campbell and
Michael Martin.

In what follows, we are going to find that there are many unusual
aspects to Disjunctivism. But perhaps the single most astounding aspect is this: it is clear in the literature that the authors think that commonality is a *hypothesis*. Some people think that the experience in the
good case and the experience in the bad case can be the same, others
deny this. And then there are endless discussions about whether or
not one is accurate in introspecting one's own experiences, whether

---

5. Byrne, Alex, and Heather Logue, eds. *Disjunctivism: Contemporary Readings.* Cambridge,
MA: MIT Press, 2009,. ix.

indiscriminability proves sameness, and whether the non-transitivity of impressions of indiscriminability shows that the commonality thesis is wrong. (The non-transitivity comes out in the following sort of experiment: the subject cannot discriminate A from B and cannot discriminate B from C, but can discriminate A from C.) I think all of these discussions are misconceived. In philosophy (unlike neuroscience), the idea that there can be hallucinations that have the same phenomenology and the same intentional content as the veridical experience is not a hypothesis, it is a *stipulation*. We just decide as a thought experiment to stipulate not only that there are hallucinations and veridical experiences that are indiscriminable, but that they are indiscriminable for the reason that they have exactly the same phenomenological features. We will confine our discussion to cases where the phenomenology fixes the intentional content. If the phenomenology is one of seeming to see something red, then the intentional content is that the subject is seeing something red. All of the discussions about the non-transitivity of indiscriminability and the possibility of being mistaken about one's own introspective data are simply beside the point. When Descartes postulated the possibility of an evil demon, he had not done a lot of empirical studies of evil demons and found that they had the capacity to produce hallucinations that are the same as veridical experiences. He postulated it as a thought experiment. In order to refute that, one would have to show not that one can be mistaken about one's own experiences (that one has only limited capacity to discriminate, that indiscriminability is non-transitive, etc.), but that it is somehow conceptually and logically impossible that a veridical experience should be the same as a corresponding hallucination. The situation logically is as follows: Grant me that it is at least possible that there can be two subjective perceptual experiences, one of which is hallucinatory and the other veridical, each one of which has some phenomenology (it need not be a phenomenology in common). If you grant that as a mere possibility, then it is possible, for philosophical purposes, to stipulate that we will consider cases where the phenomenology and the intentional content are exactly the same in the two cases. All the other empirical features that one reads in the literature about our inability to discriminate what are in fact different perceptions, the non-transitivity of indiscriminability, etc., are simply irrelevant. We are stipulating commonality.

The situation is something like the famous case of the schoolteacher who says, "Let X be the number of sheep," to which a philosophically minded child says, "But teacher, suppose X is not the number of sheep." There are even discussions about whether the burden of proof of Disjunctivism or commonality is on the Disjunctivists or the commonality theorists. Does the teacher have to prove that X is the number of sheep? In order to refute the commonality thesis, you would have to show that it is logically impossible that there could be a common phenomenology. It is not enough to argue that one might be mistaken in any given case or that judgments of indiscriminability are non-transitive. Commonality is not a hypothesis, it is a stipulation.

As with all such stipulations, there are grounds for making the stipulation. In the case of the sheep, we assume that sheep are countable using the natural numbers, and that, for example, "the square root of minus seven" is not a possible answer to the question, "How many sheep?" In the case of hallucinations, it is at least *possible* that there should be a hallucination that had some phenomenology. If it has any phenomenology at all, then as a thought experiment let us consider cases where two token different experiences are in fact type identical. If you grant me that it is possible for there to be phenomenologically identical experiences, and if for at least some features, the basic features, the phenomenology is sufficient to fix the intentional content, then a common phenomenology implies a common intentional content.

If, like me, you have never had a hallucination, it might be useful to think also of dreams where the conscious subjective components of the dream clearly exist independently of any external objects perceived.

Well, if we can treat commonality as a stipulation, why could not the Disjunctivists equally well stipulate Disjunctivism? That is, why could they not stipulate a sense of "perceptual experience" where the perceptual experiential component is individuated by whether or not there actually is an object of perception? In such a case, you simply stipulate that the perceptual experience is different in good and bad cases. I think if you look at all closely at the literature, this is in fact exactly what is going on. Consider the following from Michael Martin about having a veridical perception. He says: "No experience like this, no experience of fundamentally the same kind, could occur had no appropriate object for awareness existed."[6] How does he know? This is a stunning claim. It is explicitly denied by neuroscientific research on hallucination.[7] On the face of it, what is in common between the hallucination and the indiscriminable identical good case is that they share an identical phenomenology and therefore, for at least a certain range of features, an identical intentional content. Martin stipulates that they cannot be "of fundamentally the same kind." What is supposed to be added by "fundamentally"? Martin and other Disjunctivists in question have not done a careful study of the psychology and the neurobiology of perceptual experience to discover that they are radically different in the two sorts of cases. They have, for philosophical reasons, decided to treat them as radically different. This is why there is so much unclarity about what exactly is said to be *not in common* between the good and the bad cases. The

---

6. Martin, M. G. F. "The Limits of Self-Awareness," in Byrne and Logue. *Disjunctivism: Contemporary Readings*, 279.

7. ffytche, Howard, Brammer, Woodruff, and Williams. "The Anatomy of Conscious Vision."

actual strategy is to stipulate that perceptual experiences are individuated by whether or not they are veridical. The Disjunctivists begin with the common-sense distinction between veridical and non-veridical perceptions. So far so good. But, having made the decision to individuate perceptual *experiences,* they are then forced to say there is some difference in the experience itself between the good and the bad cases, *some difference beyond the fact that one is veridical and the other not.* There is an obvious difference between the good and the bad cases—one is good and the other is bad. But the Disjunctivists want to insist that there must be something beyond that. There must be something more than just the fact that in the one case I am seeing the object, and in the other I am having an experientially type identical hallucination of the object.

It is important to understand this point exactly. I, along with Descartes and just about everybody else, by stipulation decide to consider cases of veridical experience and cases of corresponding hallucinations that are exactly the same. Disjunctivists, again by stipulation, decide to individuate perceptual experiences by whether or not they are veridical. Both sides have to agree that conscious qualitative subjective states really exist. Without conscious subjectivity there is no possibility of discussing the issues.[8] The theory that I am advancing, conscious presentational intentionality, individuates these experiences by their phenomenology and therefore for the basic cases, by their intentional content. Again, the Disjunctivists individuate the

8. Campbell, though he continues to use the vocabulary of "consciousness," actually implies that conscious perceptual experiences do not exist. That is, in the sense I and just about everybody else uses the expression "consciousness" to refer to states that have a "what- it-feels-like" feature. He does not acknowledge the existence of such conscious perceptual states. He says the *only* features of the perceptual situation are the perceiver, the object, and the point of view. In response to an earlier draft of this chapter, he points out that he does not explicitly deny the existence of perceptual consciousness. Quite so, but if there are only three features, all of them ontologically objective, there is no room for ontologically subjective perceptual consciousness. More about his views later.

conscious perceptual experiences by whether or not they are veridical. The Disjunctivists' stipulation, however, has a much greater commitment than the commonality thesis stipulation. The commonality stipulation requires only that it be possible for there to be two perceptual experiences, one good, one bad, with exactly the same phenomenology and the same intentional content. The Disjunctivists' stipulation requires that in addition to the fact that one is good and the other bad, there must be some further difference in every case. But on their view, it is impossible that there could be two cases, one good, one bad, with exactly the same phenomenology and intentional content.

Having made that stipulation, the Disjunctivist is then committed to providing us with careful descriptions of the conscious components of the veridical experience and of the hallucinatory experience that will show that in every case they must be different. I have not seen any Disjunctivist seriously attempt to do this, so let us go to the next deep question. Why would anyone want to make this stipulation? Martin gives a clear answer. He believes that if you do not make this stipulation you are forced to deny Naïve or Direct Realism. As Martin writes, "The prime reason for endorsing disjunctivism is to block the rejection of a view of perception I'll label *Naïve Realism*. The Naïve Realist thinks that some at least of our sensory episodes are presentations of an experience-independent reality."[9] If you grant the commonality assumption, then the "highest common factor" would be the object of perception. I actually think that this is the only serious argument I have seen for Disjunctivism[10] as I have defined it, and the reader by now will recognize it as the Bad Argument. However, I am going to say much more about it in detail later. The deep motivation for Disjunctivism is the conviction that there is a high philosophical

---

9. Byrne and Logue. *Disjunctivism: Contemporary Readings*, 272.

10. Martin has another argument about imagination, and I will discuss it briefly later.

price to be paid for the commonality thesis, and one sees this in one author after another. I am going to argue in the rest of this chapter that there is no price at all to be paid for the commonality thesis *once you have an adequate account of the presentational intentionality of perceptual experience.* Ironically, the very formulation that Martin uses to express his view is the formulation I would use to characterize my view, which constitutes a rejection of his Disjunctivism. He says, "some at least of our sensory episodes are *presentations* of an *experience-independent reality*" (my italics). This states my view exactly.

II. ARGUMENTS IN FAVOR OF DISJUNCTIVISM AND REPLIES TO THEM

The most common argument is a variation of the Bad Argument that says the commonality thesis has the consequence that Naïve Realism is false. But Naïve Realism is true, so commonality is false. Suppose there were a common feature to the good and the bad cases, a "highest common factor" to use McDowell's phrase. If so, the highest common factor would be the object of perception, an ontologically subjective entity that is perceived. But then if that is true, Naïve Realism is false. We know independently that Naïve Realism is true, so by contraposition the highest common factor theory must be false. The Bad Argument in its traditional form makes it out that the highest common factor is the object perceived, the sense datum. This argument denies the first premise that there is a highest common factor, and consequently preserves Naïve Realism by accepting the validity of the argument while challenging its soundness on the grounds that the first premise is false. So both the sense datum theorists and the Disjunctivists make the same mistake, though they think they are arguing with each other. The mistake is to suppose that the commonality thesis implies that the common element is perceived in both the veridical and the hallucinatory case.

Throughout this book I have argued for a form of Direct Realism that is not only consistent with the commonality thesis, but is in fact a direct consequence of the account of the presentational intentionality of perception that I provided in Chapter 2. It is at this point that the disagreement between me and the Disjunctivist comes up most strongly. I think that commonality does not refute Direct Realism and that it is the Bad Argument to suppose that it does.

I said that the Disjunctivists are mistaken in thinking you have to pay any price at all for accepting the commonality thesis. I am going to list the things that they think are the price of accepting commonality and then show in every case that you do not have to pay that price. Suppose someone accepted two of the major claims of this book, first, that the Bad Argument is truly bad, and second, that genuine perception has presentational intentionality and thus implies Direct Realism. For anyone who accepts those two, there is no motive at all for accepting Disjunctivism. It becomes not so much false as just unnecessary.

Objection 1: Commonality Implies the Negation of Naïve Realism

As I said, the most common argument for Disjunctivism is that it is the only way to preserve Naïve Realism, and as it stands, this is the Bad Argument. But the issues here are so large that I want to go into them a bit further. I have argued throughout that you can have commonality and Naïve Realism once you recognize the fallaciousness of the Bad Argument. Direct Realism just says that you perceive objects directly and not by way of first perceiving something else. The visual experience is the content but not the object of perception. The Disjunctivists I know think they have a stronger sense of Naïve Realism than simply the version of Direct Realism that I have been espousing. A favorite saying of theirs is that in the veridical case the object is *literally* part of the perceptual experience, but in the hallucinatory case there is no object as part of the perceptual experience; so the perceptual experiences are "fundamentally" different in the two cases. So far, I have not answered this conception of Naïve Realism.

REPLY TO OBJECTION 1

Let us consider the claim that the object is literally part of the perceptual experience. There is a way of interpreting this claim such that it is trivially true and another way of interpreting in which it is trivially false. If you look at the truth conditions of "the subject S sees object O," it is obvious that the occurrence of "O" is extensional; that is, the truth of the statement implies the existence of O. And in that sense the object is part of the total set of truth conditions of the statement, so the claim is trivially true. But there is another sense in which it is trivially false, because the physical object seen cannot literally be a piece of the subjective perceptual experience in the head.

But there is also a deeper sense in which the object is a constitutive part, and that is precisely because the form of the experience is that of presentational intentionality. The conditions will not be satisfied unless the intentionality reaches right up to the object and unless the object causes the experience of it. Remember, perception is not just a *representation*, but a direct *presentation*. So once again, direct perception is not an argument in favor of Disjunctivism; rather, it is a natural consequence of the presentational intentionality of perception.

There is a subjective component in any conscious perception. In the case of vision, the subjective experience is in the head of the perceiver and the object is not in her head. But in my experience, the Disjunctivists believe that they have a stronger sense of the concept of Naïve Realism, where the object is literally part of the experience. This claim is neither trivially true nor trivially false. What exactly could they mean? All of these are actual events and objects that occur in space-time in the real world. There is an object out there. There is a subjective experience going on in my head. And the subjective experience is caused by the impact of light reflected off the object onto my photoreceptor cells. I have drawn a picture in Chapter 1 of how these entities relate to each other. I think the relations are clearly depicted in that chapter, but anyone who challenges my picture has to draw me another one. It is not easy to see how the Disjunctivists can draw a coherent picture of the perceptual situation, because the constraints on the picture are:

(a) Light reflected off an object causes a sequence of neuron firings beginning at the photo receptor cells of the retina.

(b) That sequence eventually produces a *conscious visual experience.*

(c) Like all conscious states, these conscious visual experiences are qualitative, ontologically subjective, and part of a unified conscious field. They never come just in isolation, but are part of a totality of my consciousness at any time.

(d) They are all in the head; that is, the impact of the photons eventually causes qualitative, subjective visual experiences and like all other biological phenomena, such as photosynthesis and digestion, these exist entirely in the biological system. They exist in systems of cells—in this case, neurons—and there is no way that they could, so to speak, leak outside the brain and be floating around the neighboring area. I will come back to this point later. This, I think, is probably my decisive objection to Disjunctivism. No sense has been given to the claim that the object is part of the perception, because no sense has been given to the claim that the conscious qualitative subjective perceptual experience, existing entirely in the head, can contain the physical object that is seen.

So we have found a third way of interpreting the claim: In addition to being either trivially true or trivially false, there is a way of understanding the claim where no clear meaning has been given to it in a way that would enable us to diagram the relations between the various entities involved. If you think that the desk is literally a part of my perceptual experience of the desk, in the same sense in which my experience of color is literally a part of my perceptual experience, draw me a picture that shows both the subjective and the objective ontologies and their causal relations.

CONTINUATION OF REPLY TO OBJECTION 1: THE ELEMENTS OF THE PERCEPTUAL SITUATION

These issues are so important that it is worth going over the diagrams again. Remember, the philosophy of visual perception begins when photons are reflected off the perceived object and the photon strike the retina and set up a series of events. The story here is both causal and intentional, but for the sake of simplicity and avoiding unnecessary arguments, I will ignore the intentionality of perception for the moment. Here (Figs. 6.1, 6.2) is what the picture looks like:

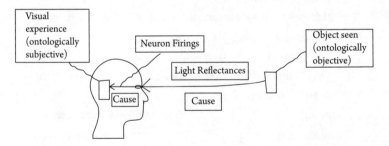

Figure 6.1. This depicts the causal sequence by which the visual perception causes a conscious visual experience in the brain.

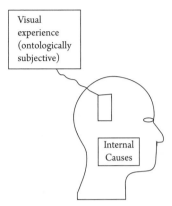

Figure 6.2. This depicts a hallucination in which a type-identical visual experience occurs without a perception of an object.

In the two cases, by stipulation, the phenomenology of the hallucinatory experience and that of the veridical experience are identical.

Now what exactly is the Disjunctivist going to say about these pictures? Remember, we are talking about real (biological) and therefore physical events in the world. That is, the touchy-feely, qualitative, subjective inner perceptual experience is simply a physical datum of biology. Its existence is not something that is worth arguing about, though of course I am prepared to argue for it. Anybody who has a theory of perception has to be able to draw these pictures, because there are spatial and causal relations between the different entities involved and they must be describable. Remember also that the visual experience is not itself seen because in the veridical case it is precisely the *seeing* of the object perceived, and in the hallucinatory case it is a conscious perceptual experience that has no object.

I will describe two accounts because I have had a chance to discuss them with their authors and so I feel more confident in my representation. I know them better than I know other accounts of Disjunctivism. The first is the relational theory associated with John Campbell. On the relational theory, there are three and only three elements in the perceptual situation: the perceiver, the object, and the point of view. There is nothing in his account that acknowledges the existence of a conscious, qualitative subjective perceptual experience going on in the head of the perceiver. He is committed to denying the view that gets the subject going in the first place. The essential question cannot be posed: What exactly are the relations between the ontologically subjective conscious experience and the ontologically objective objects seen? Furthermore, there is no answer on this view to the question: What exactly does the impact of the photons on the photoreceptor cells cause? This is not only mistaken philosophy, it is mistaken neurobiology, because without giving any reason, it denies the standard neurobiological accounts of how visual perception occurs. (For a standard account, see Christof Koch's *The Quest for Consciousness: A Neurobiological Approach.*[11]) I do not know how to draw the picture of hallucinations on this account. It seems to me there are four decisive objections to the "relational" account:

1. It does not account for hallucinations.
2. It cannot give a causal account of what happens after the photons hit the photoreceptor cells.
3. It implicitly denies the existence of conscious perceptual experiences; that is, it denies the existence of qualitative, subjective perceptual states.
4. It cannot distinguish the same content in different modalities so both seeing the smoothness of the table and feeling the smoothness of the table relate the perceiver to the smoothness of the table; but the subjective quality of seeing is quite different from the subjective quality of feeling. I do not see how the relational theory can state these facts. I will come back to this point later.

11. Koch. *The Quest for Consciousness: A Neurobiological Approach.*

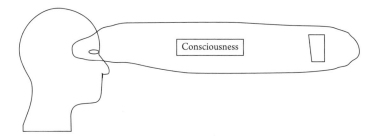

Figure 6.3. This depicts how some Disjunctivists think of the conscious perceptual experience as including the object perceived as a part. I argue that this makes no sense.

There are lots of other objections in addition to these four, but each of these seems decisive, so perhaps they are enough. I will make further objections to Campbell's account later in this chapter when I consider the conscious aspect of conscious perception.

A second view, which may be associated with Michael Martin and Alva Noë, is that somehow or other in the veridical case, the consciousness goes outside the head and envelops the object itself. Frankly, I do not think such a view can be made coherent, but let us try it. The consciousness we are talking about is a biological phenomenon; that is, it is qualitative, it is ontologically subjective, and it always exists as part of a total conscious field. Like all biological phenomena, in real life it is realized in cellular systems. Think of photosynthesis, digestion, or lactation as comparable biological phenomena. None of these can just float around in space. All biology has to be realized in physical, biological systems. But suppose we created an artificial visual consciousness outside of biological systems. Surely such a thing is logically possible and may even be technologically possible someday. Fine. All the same, the consciousness still has to be realized in something. This is a general feature of all higher-level features in the real world—the solidity of the table, the liquidity of the water, the elasticity of the steel bar. All higher-level physical phenomena are realized in physical substrates. What exactly is the physical substrate when the consciousness leaks outside the brain? I am embarrassed to have to ask these questions because asking the question already exposes the implausibility of the theory under examination. (I am presupposing that the Cartesian view, that qualitative subjective consciousness is not a physical feature of the real biological world, is out of the question. We have had over three centuries of failure to make any sense of that view.) But the bottom line, as my students would say, of this discussion is that the Disjunctivist conception of perception is not so much false as incoherent because no coherent account is given of the spatial and causal relationships between the object perceived, the conscious experience of it, and other elements of the environment such as the brain of the perceiver. It is a condition of adequacy on anybody's theory of perception that they be able to present these relationships and show how veridical and hallucinatory cases relate to each other.

Objection 2: A Disjunctive Argument for Disjunctivism

Michael Martin has an argument that he thinks is not subject to the objections I have made to the Bad Argument. I think it is, but it is worth spelling it out. He considers the view, which he and I both accept, and which he calls, Experiential Naturalism. That is roughly the idea that our experiences are part of the natural world and subject to the causal order. He thinks that Experiential Naturalism, together with the commonality thesis—what he calls "The Common Kind Assumption"—forces the rejection of Naïve Realism. Here is how the argument goes:

> So, Experiential Naturalism imposes certain constraints on what can be true of hallucinatory experiences. Such experiences either can have only experience-dependent objects, *or not be relations to*

objects at all. By the Common Kind Assumption, whatever is true of the kind of experience that one has when one is hallucinating, the same must be true of the kind of experience one has when perceiving. So either one's experience when veridically perceiving is of some mind-dependent object, or the experience is not essentially a relation to any object at all.[12]

REPLY TO OBJECTION 2

The crucial sentence is this, "By the common kind assumption, whatever is true of the kind of experience one has when one is hallucinating, the same must be true of the kind of experience one has when one is perceiving." This sentence is ambiguous. It can mean that what is true of the ontologically subjective qualitative character of the good case must be true of the bad case as well. This is indeed a requirement and is met by the commonality assumption as I have presented it. But it could also mean that whatever relation to objects the two cases have must be the same, and that immediately produces an absurdity because the bad case is not a relation to an object at all. That is what is meant by calling it a hallucination. There is one thing that by stipulation is obviously not true of the two experiences: One is veridical and the other is not. One involves the perception of a mind-independent object, the other involves no such perception. The Common Kind Assumption requires only that the actual inner qualitative character of the experience be the same in the two cases, which it is. But this is not inconsistent with the fact that one is veridical and the other one is not. But I would not wish to be too swift, so let us go over it again.

Let us consider each of Martin's two disjuncts. I think it is obvious that in the hallucination there is no object. That is part of the

---

12. Martin, "The Limits of Self-Awareness" in Byrne & Logue eds: p. 275.

definition of a hallucination, and it is the Bad Argument to suppose there must be a sense datum as an object. The veridical experience is a relation to an object that is seen. A hallucinatory experience has no object. What is the problem supposed to be? To repeat, here is the crucial claim. The Common Kind Assumption requires us to postulate that "whatever is true of the kind of experience that one has when one is hallucinating, the same must be true of the kind of experience one has when perceiving. So either one's experience when veridically perceiving is of some mind-dependent object, or the experience is not essentially a relation to any object at all." I believe this claim exhibits precisely the failure to distinguish between content and object which underlies the Bad Argument. I agree with Martin that it is not simply a repetition of the Bad Argument, but it is a repetition of the basic principle that gives rise to the Bad Argument, namely same *content* implies same *object*. That would be the Bad Argument. Let me emphasize this point: Experiential Naturalism does not have the consequence that the commonality between the good and the bad cases implies that each has the same object. That would be a false conclusion, because the whole point of distinguishing good and bad cases is to distinguish those that have an object and those that do not. Why would anyone suppose that they must have the same *object*? I cannot say this often enough: Same content does not imply same object. I look at the desk and see the desk, so my experience has the desk as object. I have a hallucination which has exactly the same content and no object. The conjunction of Experiential Naturalism and the Common Kind Assumption does not state that the same content implies the same object. On the contrary, the only reason we focus on these cases is that they illustrate the point that in two perceptual experiences you can have exactly the same intentional content with an intentional object in one case and no intentional object in the other case.

Objection 3: The Epistemic Argument

In the literature, it is common to distinguish between metaphysical and epistemic Disjunctivism. I have so far concentrated my attention on metaphysical Disjunctivists such as Campbell and Martin. But there is a separate epistemic argument for Disjunctivism, an argument for distinguishing two kinds of experiences, which I have so far ignored. I do not think it is an argument for Disjunctivism as I have defined it, but let us state the argument and see what we find.

In veridical perception we get direct knowledge of the world around us. If the commonality thesis were correct, there would be some additional component in the perceptual situation, and it is hard to see how a correct account of the epistemology could be given. The conception of perception on the commonality thesis is that veridical perception is simply additive. You take hallucination and add to it the object causing the hallucination, and that gives you a veridical perception. This is an absurd picture of perception and it makes it impossible to account for the direct knowledge that we get from perceptual experience.

In John McDowell's reply to Tyler Burge,[13] he says that regarding the sort of experiences that he is considering, "[s]ome aspect of objective reality is *there* for a subject, perceptually *present* to her. That is a more demanding condition than experience's being merely veridical." He goes on to say that "to have an experience describable in those terms is to have an *indefeasible* warrant for believing that things are as the experience is revealing them to be."

13. McDowell, John. "Tyler Burge on Disjunctivism." *Philosophical Explorations* 13 (2010): 3, 243–55.

REPLY TO OBJECTION 3

McDowell's description sounds very much like my own view except for the metaphor of "indefeasible." He uses the same concept of "presence" that I am using. So, for example, as I look at the table on which I am now working, it is directly present to me, in a sense I think that he is driving at, and that is stronger than mere veridicality because I might have a veridical perception of something very faint in the distance. But there is nothing faint about the presence of the table. As McDowell and I agree, it is perceptually present to me. And, phenomenologically speaking, in this situation it would be very hard for me to doubt that the table was actually here, so that much in his account seems to me right. The problem is this: The phenomenology of direct presentation by itself does not guarantee success. I take it the point that Burge was making, and one I agree with, is that you could have exactly this presentational phenomenology and still be mistaken. McDowell draws an analogy with a free-throw shooter where the shooter has a fallible capacity, but that does not mean that every case could be a failure. On the contrary, some of them are known to be successful. But the analogy is weak because the actual analogy is not with *successfully* shooting a free throw, but with *trying* to shoot a free throw with the phenomenology of trying, and any effort of trying could fail even though many do not. Similarly, the phenomenology of perceptual experience, of having such experiences, by itself is insufficient to guarantee success even though most are successful.

I think the picture he has of the alternative view is a mistaken conception of the commonality assumption. He seems to think that the alternative view treats visual experiences as if they were like pains. One might have the same kind of pain, sometimes caused by an external object and sometimes not. But the commonality thesis does not imply the conception of perception as arrived at by the *addition* of independent elements precisely because the visual experience has intrinsic intentionality. The visual experience is a *direct* presentation of the object and states of affairs perceived. They are not something added onto it. The commonality thesis, as I present it, emphasizes the presentational intentionality of perception. The veridical case is the case precisely where the object that causes the experience is the intentional object of the experience itself. The form of causation is intentional causation. The account of the epistemology of direct perception—which I think is correct—is found, for example, in Stroud.[14] It is a consequence of the presentational intentionality that I have been expounding. It is definitely *not* an argument for Disjunctivism.

Objection 4: Perceptual Experience as an Interface

On the commonality thesis, the perceptual experience would be an interface between the perceiver and the object perceived. This view is advanced even by some philosophers who reject Disjunctivism. For example, Tim Crane, who is not a Disjunctivist, writes:

> In a certain sense, then, critics of intentionalism are right when they say that on the intentionalist view, perception "falls short" of the world, and in this sense creates what Putnam calls an "interface" between the mind and the world. The essence of perception— perceptual experience itself—does fall short of the world. But, according to the intentionalist, this is not something which should create any metaphysical or epistemological anxiety; it is simply a consequence of a general aspect of intentionality as traditionally conceived.[15]

14. Stroud, Barry. "Seeing What Is So," in *Perception, Causation, and Objectivity,* ed. Johannes Roessler, Hemdat Lerman, and Naomi Eilan. Oxford: Oxford University Press, 2011, 92–102.
15. Crane, Tim. "Is There a Perceptual Relation?," in *Perceptual Experience,* ed. Tamar Szabo Gendler and John Hawthorne. Oxford: Clarendon Press, 2006, 141.

REPLY TO OBJECTION 4

This is a stunning passage. I believe it gives a mistaken account of the intentionality of perception and I see no alternative but to go through it step-by-step.

1. Crane tells us, "critics of intentionalism are right when they say that on the intentionalist view perception falls short of the world." My reply to this objection is that I do not know whose account of Intentionality he has in mind but on the kind of Intentionality that I have been advocating since 1983, perception precisely does not "fall short" of the world. On my account of "intentionalism," when I grab the table I actually grab the table. When I see the table, I actually see the table.

2. "The essence of perception—the perceptual experience itself—does fall short of the world." *The very essence of perception falls short of the world.* This is exactly the opposite of the view that I have been advancing of the relationship between perception and reality. One has to ask, what would perception be like if it did not fall short of the world? And I think the answer is that it would be exactly as it is now, not falling short of the world.

3. This falling short of the world is what Putnam calls an "interface" between the mind and the world. Anyone who says this should tell us exactly what is meant by "interface." Is there supposed to be some entity that gets between me and the object when I see it and is this the "interface"? It is perhaps not surprising that Crane, who is not a Disjunctivist, does not tell us exactly about the nature of the interface. He does not tell us why perception does not actually reach what it is supposed to be reaching, but only by way of an "interface."

4. He comforts us with the idea that this does not create "any metaphysical or epistemological anxiety." It is simply a consequence of the generalized aspect of intentionality as traditionally conceived. I wish he had told us exactly what the tradition is. In the book I mentioned earlier, I emphasized the *presentational intentionality* of both perceptual experiences and intentions-in-action.

The visual experience is not an interface. An interface, I suppose, would be an entity that gets between the perceiver and the object perceived. But in fact, the visual experience *just is* the perception of the object. It is not an interface, or an interfacing entity, or anything of the sort. Suppose somebody said that whenever I hit a nail with a hammer there is an interface between the hammer and the nail, namely my hitting. But the hitting is not an interface. It is just what happens when I hit the nail. It is the hitting of the nail in the same way visual experience is the seeing of the object. An interface would be a separate entity that is itself perceived. And that, of course as we have seen over and over, is the Bad Argument. You cannot perceive the visual experience because it is the perceiving. It is not an interface, it is the perceiving itself.

As usual, you can see these points quite clearly if you consider touch. Rub your hand along the surface of the table and you have a sensation of the smoothness of the tabletop. But that sensation is not an interface between you and the table. Rather, it is your way of feeling the table itself.

The most disappointing feature of Crane's account is that it makes it seem that somehow or other Disjunctivism is intellectually respectable. As if you pay a price for intentionalism and you pay a price for Disjunctivism, but reasonable philosophers might decide to pay either price. I think this is a misconception. I do not think anyone can seriously entertain Disjunctivism if they are possessed of an adequate theory of the intentionality of perception.

Objection 5: Sense Data

A fifth argument against the commonality thesis is that it would have perception providing us with a *"datum"* or "ground" on the basis of which we know about the world. Whereas in fact, what it provides us with is direct knowledge.

REPLY TO OBJECTION 5

This is really the same mistake repeated over and over again. The visual experience is in no sense a "datum," "evidence," "ground," or anything else on the basis of which one knows that there is an object there. Rather, in veridical perception seeing and knowing are the same. You just know that the object is thereby seeing it. Stroud makes this very point.[16] But it is perfectly consistent with (indeed it follows from) the presentational conception of the intentionality of perceptual experience.

Objection 6: Veridical Perception Is Transparent or Diaphanous

The veridical case of the perception reaches right up to the object itself. We see right through to the object, we do not see any intermediate entities, and the description of our perception is precisely a description of the object in the external world. *If you try to describe your experience, you end up describing the objects and states of affairs that you perceive.* It seems to follow from the fact that there is only one description of what is going on that there is only one thing there. There are not two independent entities, the experience and the object. The experience is transparent or diaphanous and goes right through to

16. Stroud, "Seeing What Is So."

the object. Any alternative account of perception would leave this out and consequently we have to accept Disjunctivism.

REPLY TO OBJECTION 6

What I am going to say about this argument is obvious, and I have said it in earlier chapters. The source of the transparency is precisely the presentational intentional content of the visual experience. The presentational intentional content is, "I am seeing a green table." The fact in the world that corresponds to that is that there is a green table there. What could be more obvious? *Transparency is not an argument for Disjunctivism, it is an argument against it. In fact, it is the single most powerful argument against it* because the transparency requires explanation and the Disjunctivist has nothing to offer by way of explanation. How can the qualitative subjective experience entirely in my head give me direct immediate presentation of ontologically objective objects and states of affairs in the world? The answer is that the experience has presentational intentionality of precisely the sort that I have described.

Transparency is a problem for the Disjunctivists, and I want to say exactly why. The transparency comes out of this if I say:

(1) I see the green table.

If I want to capture the subjective component of that event, I might say:

(2) I seem to see the green table.

But there are different ways in which (2) might be true, so let us make it explicit which we have in mind. That is:

(3) I am having a conscious visual experience in my head
which is exactly as if I were seeing the green table.

Any conscious perceptual experience of the form (1) is going to allow
for formulations like (3), but (3) is the source of the transparency.
The description of the visual experience corresponds, more or less, exactly to the description of the state of affairs perceived. That fact
requires explanation. Typically in my experience, Disjunctivists cannot
see that an explanation is necessary.

But the argument from diaphanousness is overestimated because
of the concentration on vision. My visual experience of seeing that
the table is smooth is difficult to separate from the smoothness of the
table. But if I rub my hand over the smooth surface and feel that it is
smooth, I can easily distinguish the feeling of smoothness in my fingertips from the actual smoothness of the table. Visual experience is
not a bodily sensation, so it is possible to make the confusion
between the content of the visual experience and its conditions of satisfaction in the world. But it is much harder to make that confusion
when you are actually talking about bodily sensations, such as feeling
the smoothness of the table in your fingers and palm. I will return to
this point in the next section when I discuss Campbell's theory.

III. CONSCIOUSNESS AND PERCEPTION:
CAMPBELL'S ACCOUNT

The best way for me to explain and appraise Campbell's conception
of perception is to contrast it with my own. My account of my own
will be very brief.

Suppose I am standing in front of two square pieces of canvas,
one entirely green and the other blue, so I can see both the blue and
the green in the same conscious experience. How does it work? First,

light reflected off the canvas sets up a sequence of neurobiological processes that eventually result in the conscious experiences of both green and blue. These experiences have intrinsic Intentionality—that is to say, I could not have them without them at least seeming to me that I am seeing something green and blue. They are ontologically subjective; they are qualitative and they go on in my head. If the experiences are veridical, then they are caused in the right way by the presence of the features in the objects in front of me. It is important to re-emphasize that neither experience is seen, and that neither is green nor blue. This is because they are the *seeing* of green and blue. You cannot see the seeing, and the seeing of the colors is not itself colored. This is not a very complicated story and it is one that is consistent with what we know about how the world works, both from our own experiences and from neurobiology.

What exactly is Campbell's account of the same scene? When I stand and look at these two objects, on his account, there is no qualitative subjective consciousness at all. There is just the presence of the two objects and my "conscious" perception consists of a direct relation between me and the objects. The components of the relation are simply the point of view, myself and the two objects. The "consciousness" consists entirely in this relation. Thus three essential features of my account are all denied by Campbell. They are:

(i) There are conscious, qualitative, subjective experiences going on in my head when I consciously see anything.
(ii) These are caused by the objects I am seeing.
(iii) They have intrinsic Intentionality.

Campbell denies all that. Why? As far as I can tell, his only argument is transparency. If I try to focus my attention on the visual experience, it seems I typically end up concentrating on the features of the objects. The description of the visual experience and the description of its conditions of satisfaction are typically the same, so it seems to him there must be only one phenomenon going on. I agree with the data of transparency, but I think that transparency is the problem, and not the solution. What is the explanation for the transparency? It seems obvious to me that there are two phenomena going on here, as is shown by the fact that if I close my eyes, the conscious visual experience ceases but the object perceived does not cease. This is because there is obviously something different in my conscious subjective experience from the actual objective features perceived. Why should they have the same description? Why should it even seem possible to confuse the one with the other? And the answer is obvious from everything I have said in this book. The ontologically subjective conscious experience has the ontologically objective features of the world as its conditions of satisfaction. The former is a direct presentation of the latter.

Campbell's account seems immediately false because any normal conscious perceiver has a conscious experience of green and blue, and this involves much more than just registering the presence of the two colors. A color-blind person who perceives only in shades of grey might learn to perceive the distinction between green and blue by the distinction in the shades of grey. I cannot see how Campbell can account for this case, because he denies the existence of the "private" qualitative subjective experiences which are the essences of conscious perception.

I think Campbell's account is obviously false on its face, but philosophers love arguments and I am no exception. So what arguments can I present to show that his account inadequate? I do not think it is very hard to state several such arguments, so let us do it. I have already presented one about the distinction between normal color perception and the color-blind registering of color distinctions. Here is a second, even more powerful argument. Suppose I am looking at the surface of a table. I see the smoothness of the table and it sets up a sequence of events in me that causes the conscious experience of the smoothness. Now let us suppose I run my hand along the same surface and feel the very same smoothness that I am seeing. I do not see how anyone in his right mind can deny that the conscious experience of smoothness in my fingertips is an actual conscious experience distinct from the smoothness of the object. No one can say that the smoothness in the object and the feeling of the smoothness in my fingertips are one and the same thing. A simple proof is given when I lift my fingertips and the feeling of smoothness stops, but the smoothness itself does not stop.

Why is not the same thing obvious about the visual experience? The visual experience is quite different from the quality perceived because, as I mentioned earlier, when I close my eyes the visual experience stops and the quality does not stop. The visual experience in my head is thus not identical with the qualities that I am perceiving. A difference between tactile experiences and visual experiences is that tactile experiences are *sensations* and visual experiences are not. The sensation of smoothness is a bodily sensation. It is possible to have the illusion in the case of visual experiences that they somehow contrast with tactile experiences because they are not sensations with an experienced bodily location in the way that the sensation of smoothness is indeed a conscious sensation in my fingertips.

What is the proof that both vision and touch must be treated the same way? Notice that the visual experience in which I see the smoothness and the tactile experience in which I touch the smoothness are part of one and the same total conscious experience. In this particular case, I do not have two independent experiences. I have one constant conscious field that contains both the experience of visually perceived smoothness and the experience of tactilely perceived smoothness. What stands to my visual experience as its conditions of satisfaction is exactly the same as what stands to my tactile experience as its conditions of satisfaction. In both cases I am perceiving smoothness, one case tactilely, and the other case visually. Suppose that at the same time I feel a slight pain in my back. I would then have one single constant conscious field containing at least these components (no doubt it would contain lots of others as well): the visually perceived smoothness, the tactilely perceived smoothness, the pain in my back. All of these are ontologically subjective phenomena going on in my conscious field. The reason for adding pain is that it is obvious that the pain experience is ontologically subjective and I want to show that all three (tactile experience, visual experience, and pain) have exactly the same subjective ontology, because they are all parts of a single conscious field.

Campbell's account is by no means intuitively appealing. What arguments does he present for it? As I said earlier, he relies on one argument, the argument from transparency, which he attributes to Moore. On the subject of qualitative character of the conscious experience, he cites with approval an argument from Moore, "[b]ut Moore emphatically does make the point that there is no reason to think there are intrinsic features of experience that differentiate the experience of blue from the experience of green. There is no need to appeal to either the notion of a representation of color differentiating the experiences or the notion of intrinsic sensational feature of the experience differentiating the two color experiences. The objects, blue in one case, green in the other, adequately differentiate the experiences." I do not know if this is a correct interpretation of Moore, but in any case it seems to me mistaken and I hope I have shown why with the previous examples where we had the experience of color, the experience of smoothness (both tactile and visual experiences), and pain as part of a single unified conscious field.

But this leads to another extraordinary claim by Campbell, that the "phenomenal character" of the experiences is just the actual physical qualities of the objects. In the conscious visual perception there are typically at least three elements. There is the object or the state of affairs perceived, the conscious visual experience by way of which the object is perceived, and the causal relation by way of which the object causes the conscious visual experience. Here is what Campbell says about the "phenomenal character" of experience, "On a Relational View, the phenomenal character of your experience, as you look around the room, is constituted by the actual layout of the room itself: which particular objects are there, their intrinsic properties, such as color and shape, and how they are arranged in relation to one another and to you."[17] This is a stunning claim, so let us examine it closely in light of examples we have already stated. Look around the room. You have the perceivable table, which is part of the ontologically objective visual field, and the conscious subjective experience, which is part of the subjective visual field. Initially take the sense of touch and work from that. I run my hand along the top of the table, it feels smooth. There is the smoothness of the table, which is part of the objective perceptual field, and there is the conscious sensation of smoothness in my fingertips, which is part of the subjective perceptual field. It is quite obvious that these are distinct phenomena. The objective smoothness of the table causes the subjective experience of smoothness when I run my hand along the top of it. Now, incredibly, Campbell seems to be saying that the subjective sensation of smoothness in my hand is *constituted by, and thus identical with,* the actual smoothness of the table. He says the smoothness of the table is identical with the "the phenomenal character" of your experience. That cannot be right, as is shown by the fact that when I lift my hand, the "phenomenal character" stops, but the smoothness of the table does not stop and the smoothness causes the "phenomenal character." Worse yet, the qualitative visual experience of seeing the smoothness of the table is quite different from the qualitative tactile experience of feeling the smoothness of the table. The same objective quality is perceived

17. Campbell, J. *Reference and Consciousness.* Oxford: Oxford University Press, 2002, 116.

in both cases, but the objective quality cannot be identical with the experiences because the experiences are different.

The philosophical problem of subjective qualitative perceptual experience is to try to account for how these phenomena relate to the objects perceived and much of this book has been devoted to that problem. What is Campbell's contribution to this discussion? It seems to me that he changes the subject. The subject is not the ontologically objective state of affairs perceived, but the ontologically subjective experiences going on in one's head. For him to suppose that he is addressing ontological subjectivity by identifying it with ontological objectivity is simply changing the subject. Its only connection is that the word "quality" seems to apply both to the qualities of objects and to the qualitative character of the experience. But this is just a bad pun. It is as if one had said in addressing the problem of cancer, "well, the solution to the problem of cancer is to say that 'cancer' also means crab. But crabs are not the same as cancer." The problem of the qualitative character of perception is simply not addressed by attempting to identify these with objective features of objects. They are two entirely different phenomena, related by conscious intentionality and causation. In actual perception, it is the intentionality and the causation that we need to explore to give us a solution to the problem of qualitative experience.

Campbell is committed to the denial that perceptual consciousness exists, and this is disguised from his readers by the fact that he continues to use the vocabulary while denying the existence of its referent. In a response to an earlier draft of this chapter, he points out that he does not actually say that perceptual consciousness does not exist. Quite so; what he does say is that visual perception consists of three and only three components: the perceiver, the object perceived, and the point of view. I think this commits him to the view that perceptual consciousness (I mean real consciousness: qualitative, subjective states of feeling, sentience, or awareness) does not exist. It is as if I ask somebody, "was Sally in the room?" And he says, "there were only three people in the room: Tom, Dick, and Harry." Well, he did not actually say Sally was not in the room, but on the reasonable assumption that Sally is neither Tom, Dick, nor Harry, he is committed to the view that Sally was not in the room in exactly the same way Campbell is committed to the view that qualitative, subjective conscious perceptual experiences do not exist. I do not believe you can *begin* to give an account of conscious perception with that assumption.

IV. THE REAL SOURCE OF THE DISAGREEMENT

Typically in philosophy the surface disagreements are manifestations of much larger differences that do not always appear on the surface. I think something like that is happening in this case. It looks like one class of philosophers is arguing that there is something "fundamentally" in common between the good and the bad cases, and the Disjunctivists are arguing that there is nothing "fundamentally" in common. But that apparent flat disagreement really depends on a much larger difference in the conception of perception that different philosophers have. I want to conclude this discussion not by adding a further refutation of Disjunctivism but simply by showing the price you have to pay if you deny the commonality thesis.

The real difficulty with Disjunctivism is that you cannot give a consistent and coherent account of the entities involved. Remember, as I said earlier, all these are real events in the physical world—the hallucination, the visual perception—and as such one ought to be able to depict their geography. I have tried in Chapter 1 and earlier in this chapter to do that. There is the object outside the head that causes a conscious experience inside the head. The conscious experience presents the object as its conditions of satisfaction. In the hallucination case, the stuff inside the head can be exactly the same (by stipulation), but it is not caused by the object that is its apparent conditions of satisfaction because there is no object there (again by stipulation). I have not seen a Disjunctivist account that can give a specification of the spatial and causal relations, particularly of the visual experience and its relation to the object perceived.

A good test case for anybody's theory of perception is, Can it account for the veridical perception of objects that ceased to exist millions of years ago? I now see a star through a telescope that I know ceased to exist twenty-seven million years ago. In one respect, the experience is not veridical because, again, all experiences are of the here and now, and it seems to me that the star is existing here and now when I know in fact it does not. All the same, I know that I am seeing that particular star. Now I can draw a picture of that, indeed I have drawn such a picture in this chapter. The star causes in me a visual experience. I would like to see the picture drawn by the Disjunctivists. I do not think they can draw a coherent picture. In what sense exactly for them is the star a constituent part of the experience of it? It is pretty tough to describe that for an object that ceased to exist twenty-seven million years ago.

V. DISJUNCTIVISM AND VISUAL IMAGINATION

Martin has an additional argument for Disjunctivism based on our capacity for visual imagery. I think the argument is very complex, and I will not attempt to summarize it. But as I understand it, the heart of the argument is that in forming visual imagery we are in some important sense committed to the existence of objects in the imagined scene, and this is supposed to illustrate the way in which in actual perception the object in the scene is part of the perceptual experience. I do not think this is a correct account of visual imagination, and I will now give what I think is a more adequate account.

The essential differences between forming visual images and actually seeing something are, first, that the visual image is typically much less vivid and detailed than actually seeing something; second, that the visual image is typically formed voluntarily, it is caused by the subject's intentions-in-action. In the cases we are considering, it is an intentionally formed experience. But when you actually see something, it is not in that way up to you what your experience is. Your experience is fixed by the actual features of the scene itself. Let us go through this with an example. Suppose I am given the instruction: Form a visual image of the Eiffel Tower. There is an important sense in which I am not imagining myself as part of the scene; it is just the Eiffel Tower that I imagine. Now then suppose I have a second instruction: Form a visual image which is of yourself seeing the Eiffel Tower from a specific location, Pont Alexandre III in Paris. In the second case, I am a part of the imagined scene, and what I am imagining is myself actually seeing the Eiffel Tower. Now, here comes instruction number three: Do exactly what you did in the second case, but imagine that it is a hallucination. Imagine you are standing on the bridge having a hallucination. In that case, I can imagine exactly the same content. But in the hallucination case, I am not committed, in any sense, to the existence of an object in the imagined scene, because what I am imagining is myself having a hallucination of that object. Same imagined content in the two cases, and no commitment to an object in the second case. There is a fourth case where I am again imagining myself having the same experience with the same content, but let us imagine in this case I do not know if it is a hallucination or not. I might imagine that I wonder, is it a hallucination or not? That question is left open.

The point of these examples is to illustrate that we really cannot get interesting, important conclusions out of the features of the visual imagery because the decision of what features to put into the visual image is up to us. We can have a visual image where we are committed to the existence of an object seen in the imagined scene, and a visual image with exactly the same content but no such commitment. If anything, visual imagery counts against Disjunctivism, because one can easily have two visual images that have the same content but where one is a hallucination. In case three, I imagine myself having exactly the same type of visual experience I had in the veridical case, but by stipulation, the imagined case is imagining having a hallucination. Same content exactly, but one is veridical, the other is hallucinatory. And it is up to me how I choose to imagine it.

Chapter 7

Unconscious Perception

So far, this book has been entirely dedicated to the problem of conscious perceptions. There are, however, interesting problems concerning unconscious perception, and these issues have become more pressing because of a current climate of opinion that makes it seem as if consciousness does not really matter very much. In this atmosphere, it can be made to seem that most of the most important human mental processes and activities are unconscious, and the function of consciousness, though still unclear, is more likely to be one of regulating and monitoring rather than undertaking or initiating and carrying out human activities, including such cognitive activities as perception and thought. This chapter will be primarily concerned with unconscious perception, but I will also discuss other sorts of unconscious psychological phenomena, such as unconscious actions.[1]

I. A BRIEF HISTORY OF THE UNCONSCIOUS

We do not, in either science or philosophy, have an adequate account of the relationship between consciousness and unconsciousness. What exactly is the problem? There are several problems, but the simplest way to get into them is to discuss the history of these issues. For literally

---

1. The argument of this chapter relies heavily on the account of the unconscious in Searle, John R. *The Rediscovery of the Mind*. Cambridge, MA: MIT Press, 1992.

centuries, consciousness was regarded as relatively unproblematic and the notion of unconscious mental states was regarded as puzzling or perhaps incoherent. The argument against the unconscious went as follows: Descartes and others showed mental states are essentially conscious. Indeed, it is of the essence of mental states to be conscious. The notion of an unconscious mental state would therefore be the notion of an unconscious consciousness. This is a plain self-contradiction. On the Cartesian definition of the mental, a definition that dominated intellectual life for literally centuries, there could not be any unconscious mental phenomena. As early as the nineteenth century, there were people who challenged this conception and championed the idea of unconscious mental phenomena. Three examples are Dostoevsky in literature, and Nietzsche and Schopenhauer in philosophy. Freud certainly did not invent the idea of the unconscious, but he did more to popularize it than anybody else. It is hard today to recover the enormous influence that Freud had on intellectual life. Wystan Auden characterized it this way: "To us he is no more a person/Now but a whole climate of opinion."[2] Freud's conception of the unconscious is more complex than people realize.[3] But briefly, the Freudian conception is that we need a distinction between the pre-conscious and the unconscious. The pre-conscious consists of phenomena we do not happen to be thinking about, such as my belief that Washington was the first president of the United States. But the unconscious for Freud involves cases of genuine repression. The Freudian notion of the unconscious as opposed to pre-conscious was the notion of mental states that are just too painful to emerge into consciousness. The male child's desire to have sex with his mother and to kill his father, for example, was regarded

---

2. Auden, W. H. "In Memory of Sigmund Freud." *Another Time.* New York: Random House, 1940.

3. Freud, S. "The Unconscious," in *The Standard Edition of the Complete Psychological Works of Sigmund Freud, Volume XIV (1914–1916)*. London: Hogarth Press, 1956, 159–215.

by Freud as a repressed *unconscious* form of motivation, because that desire was too painful to acknowledge but was nonetheless present as part of the child's motivation.

Freud is, I think, intellectually out of fashion today and his theory is no longer regarded as a valid scientific conception of the unconscious. But in the later decades of the twentieth century there emerged another conception of the unconscious, which I might call the Cognitive Unconscious. There were supposed to be processes going on in your brain that are genuinely mental, as opposed to merely neurobiological, but inaccessible in principle to consciousness. Of course they are *realized* or *implemented* neurobiologically. But the level of description that is essential for understanding the processes is that of the unconscious mental level, and not at either the neurobiological or the conscious level. The idea was that to explain human cognition we must postulate the existence of genuinely mental processes going on in the brain that are not conscious, not even the kind of thing that could become conscious, but all the same at a higher level than that of neurobiology. So there were supposed to be three levels of explanation: a top level of intentionality, sometimes contemptuously called "folk psychology," a bottom level of neurobiology, and an intermediate level where a Cognitive Science—as then construed—could operate.

Two examples of this tripartite conception were in vision and in the acquisition and use of language. In the case of vision, the idea was that in order to explain visual information processing, we had to postulate a computational level that is unconscious but nonetheless not just a matter of neurobiology. The classic text here is Marr's book *Vision.*[4] Marr postulated three different levels of analysis. The top level he called the computational level. This is the level at which the system solves its problems. So, for example, the visual system has to be

---

4. Marr, David. *Vision: A Computational Investigation into the Human Representation and Processing of Visual Information.* San Francisco: W. H. Freeman and Company, 1982.

able to consciously detect the shape of an object. At the bottom level there is the neurophysiology in which all of this goes on. But the unique contribution of Marr, and indeed of the whole computational conception of the mind, is to postulate an intermediate level between the top level of problem-solving and the bottom of neurobiology. At this intermediate level there are algorithms implemented by the "hardware" of the system. Why is this so important? It means that there is a science of vision that is not intentionalistic psychology and not neurobiology either. There is an intermediate level, and a science of vision could proceed at that level by figuring out the algorithms that the agent is following, by figuring out the computer programs being implemented in the brain.

It will not be a surprise to readers of this book, as well as readers of my earlier work, that I think this whole conception is confused. There is a level of intentionality, indeed, several levels, and there is a level of the neurobiological realization of the intentionality, indeed, several levels; but there is no psychologically real, but unconscious, level of algorithmic processing. The idea is that these mental processes in the intermediate level are supposed to be psychologically real, though totally unconscious. They are not the sort of thing that one could be conscious of, but they provide a scientific explanation of the operation of the visual system. No clear sense has been attached to the notion that there is any psychological reality to the level of computer implementation. You can describe the brain in computational terms, as you can describe any system whatever in computational terms. But the computational processing in question is all observer relative. Such computations are all relative to the assignment of a computational interpretation by some outside observer. Sometimes it is useful to do this; for example, you can treat the stomach as engaging in computations when it figures out how much of particular chemicals to use to attack certain digestive intakes.

The argument against there being a psychologically real level of the deep unconscious is simply that any intentionality requires aspectual shape, as I have been saying over and over throughout this book. Representation is always under some aspect or other. But what is the reality of the aspectual shape when the system is totally unconscious? What is the difference between the unconscious desire for water and the unconscious desire for H_2O, both of which may be psychologically real? An agent might not know that water is H_2O, he might mistakenly believe that H_2O is something disgusting and want water but not want H_2O. What fact about him when he is totally unconscious makes him have one desire and not the other? And the answer, I believe, is clear. We understand the notion of an unconscious mental state as the notion of something that is potentially conscious. You could ask the agent, and he could bring his desires and aversions to consciousness. But in the case of the computational level in Marr, there is no prospect of bringing this to consciousness because these are not the sort of things that could become part of conscious thought processes. (I will say more about this argument later.)

Well then, why could the brain not be like any other digital computer? Could the brain be just a computational mechanism like any other? And the answer to that is: In all such cases, the computation is relative to an observer. That does not mean the computations are unreal; on the contrary, we spend a lot of money to build and program computers that carry out the computations we wish to carry out. But it does mean that computation does not name an intrinsic—observer independent—process in the way that the electrical circuit and the electrical state transitions within the hardware are intrinsic and observer independent. Rather, the hardware is designed so that when programmed we can *interpret* it in such-and-such ways. I want to put this point emphatically: Except for such cases as a conscious agent going through an arithmetical problem and carrying out computations, computation is always observer relative.

A second example of unconscious mental phenomena that function causally in the explanation of human cognition is the acquisition and use of language. The way the child is able to use language, the way that he is able to process linguistic stimuli, and the way that he is able to produce sentences is supposed to be a matter of mental processes that are not only unconscious—but unlike the Freudian unconscious—they are not the sort of the thing that the agent could become conscious of. The mental states in question are computational states. If one were to represent them in a theory, it would have to be in a notation of a computer program or more typically as a set of technical terms used by cognitive psychologists and professional linguists. When the linguist says that the child applies the rule "move alpha," there is no implication that the child is somehow a master of the Greek alphabet. This notation is just the linguist's way of representing an unconscious mental process in the child's brain.

On this account, both vision and language acquisition are matters of computation. We are to think of mental states as essentially computational states, and the computational level goes on between the level of neurobiology and the level of "folk psychology." It is psychologically real, but not the thing that is either conscious or even accessible to consciousness.

With the cognitive revolution, a shift took place. Instead of thinking of the unconscious as puzzling or problematic and consciousness as the normal form of mental life, researchers in Cognitive Science began to think of the conscious as puzzling, mysterious, and perhaps beyond the reach of scientific investigation, whereas the unconscious became a standard mode of explanation. The explanation for this shift is that, on this paradigm, we are to think of the brain as a digital computer and the mind as a set of computer programs. With the birth of Cognitive Science, at least in the early days, there was an eagerness to produce scientifically valid modes of explanation of human cognition. But the scientific explanation should not be a matter of introspective psychology nor Behaviorism. Cognitive Science was founded, at least partly, in reaction to Behaviorism. The model that seemed overwhelmingly attractive at that time was the computational paradigm. We are to think of the brain as performing lots of computations which are at the level of the mental, and not at the level of the neurobiology; but, at the same time, they are not matters of common sense or "folk" psychology and are totally unconscious.

I have attacked the notion of unconscious mental processing that was characteristic of the early decades of Cognitive Science, and I have sketched some of the argument earlier in this chapter. I now want to expand on it a bit further. First, we distinguish between, on the one hand, the shallow or ordinary unconscious, where the unconscious mental states are, in principle, the kind of thing that we can become conscious of, and on the other hand, the deep or inaccessible unconscious, where the unconscious mental states are not even the kind of thing that the agent could become conscious of. The deep unconscious is not accessible to consciousness because the rules in question do not even have a form under which they can operate consciously. They are, for example, matters of very complex computational rules, which could be stated as a very long sequence of zeros and ones. But even that is just a theoretician's way of representing the symbol manipulation that is inaccessible to consciousness.

This conception of consciousness, the deep unconsciousness, seems to me philosophically illegitimate. I promised to develop the argument about aspectual shape, so here goes: The notion of a mental state is a notion of something that represents conditions of satisfaction, but all representation is under an aspect. That means that all representation—this includes presentations of the sort that we get in perception—have to have some aspectual shape. I see the chair from this angle but not from that angle. I want something under the description water but not under the description H_2O. All intentionality is aspectual. But when the state is totally unconscious, there are only neurobiological phenomena. There is no aspectual shape at the level of the unconscious mental state, so what sense can it make to say, "The man unconsciously wants water, but does not want H_2O"? I believe we can make sense of this by supposing that the person has a mental state that is capable of being brought to consciousness. You can bring it to consciousness by asking the question, "Do you want water"? And he says, "Yes." And ask him, "Do you want H_2O"? And he says, "No." So, we can give a clear sense of the notion of an unconscious mental state, but only in terms of accessibility, in principle, to consciousness. The person might be unable to bring an unconscious mental state to consciousness for a number of reasons—for example, repression, brain damage, or simple forgetfulness. But unconscious mental states have to be the *kind of thing* that are, in principle, accessible to consciousness, and the unconscious mental states postulated by early cognitive scientists were not. The point, for the present discussion, is that the notion of an unconscious mental state not accessible to consciousness is illegitimate because it cannot account for the aspectual shape of all intentionality.

II. SUSPICIONS ABOUT CONSCIOUSNESS

Even given the rejection of the deep unconsciousness, all the same, there has been in recent decades a suspicion about consciousness as a genuine level for understanding for human behavior and human cognition. There is a suspicion that consciousness plays only a very subsidiary role in human behavior and cognition, and that many of the crucial forms of perception and voluntary action are essentially unconscious, or they can be monitored, guided by consciousness, but their initiation is unconscious. This argument was not driven by the ideology of the computer metaphor but rather is based on solid experimental results.

I will consider several examples of these results.

1. *Blindsight*

The first, and probably the most famous, is the notion of "blindsight" initially introduced by Lawrence Weiskrantz.[5] Weiskrantz initially discovered a single patient who had a form of brain damage (in Visual Area 1), which left him effectively blind in one part of his visual field. Indeed, for the patient, that part of the visual field did not exist. In the lower left quadrant, it was as if the region were like that behind his head. It is not that he saw blackness there, but there was nothing there. Weiskrantz discovered an interesting thing. If you ask a patient to fix his eyes on the center of crossing lines on a screen in front of him and then you flash rapidly an X or an O in the lower left quadrant where he is blind, and make the flash of such brief duration that he cannot move his eyes in response to the stimulus, you discover that he can report what is going on. You have to prompt him: You ask, "What did you see?" He will say things like, "I did not see anything. As you know, I had a brain injury." (Indeed, the patients tend to become irritated with the questions.) But under prompting, the patient will say, "It seemed to me there was an X there." Or, "It seemed to me there was an O there." After a week of this, Weiskrantz's patient was getting it right over 90 percent of the time. There clearly is something of an intentional form of information being received in the portion of the patient's visual field where he is blind. Weiskrantz dubbed this phenomenon "blindsight."

This is important for our investigation for several reasons. One reason is that this experiment clearly shows that there are forms of intentional perception that are not conscious. Weiskrantz thought that the most interesting aspect of this is that it shows that there is more than one neuronal pathway in the visual system and not all of the pathways are conscious. At least one of them is unconscious.

---

5. Weiskrantz, Lawrence. *Blindsight: A Case Study Spanning 35 Years and New Developments.* Oxford: Oxford University Press, 2009.

Further research by Milner and Goodale[6] supports the idea that there is more than one visual system in the brain, and that not all of the systems are conscious.

2. The Readiness Potential

The second form of unconscious information processing was revealed by the researches initially of Deecke and Kornhuber[7] in Germany in the 1970s and then repeated by Ben Libet at the end of the twentieth century in San Francisco. Their research findings seemed to show that the initiation of action was unconscious, i.e. the action was initiated prior to the agent being conscious of what he was doing.

The experimental apparatus was set up as follows: The subject was instructed to perform some simple actions such as reaching out and pushing a button. The subject was then told to look at a clock and see exactly what instant on the clock he had decided to push the button then and there, at which point the intention-in-action began. The investigation showed that there is a time lapse of about 350 milliseconds between an increased activity in the supplementary motor area and the subject's awareness of the initiation of the action. The picture that Deecke, Kornhuber, and Libet drew from these data is that the subject's brain decides that it is going to push the button before the subject is conscious of having made up his mind, and this "readiness potential" is shown by the increased activity in the supplementary motor area. The subject then becomes aware that he is going to push the button and announces this awareness to the investigator, but in fact, the subject's consciousness is simply going along for the

---

6. Milner, David, and Mel Goodale. *The Visual Brain in Action.* Oxford: Oxford University Press, 2006.

7. Deecke, Luder, Berta Grözinger, and H. H. Kornhuber. "Voluntary Finger Movement in Man: Cerebral Potentials and Theory," in *Biological Cybernetics,* 1976.

ride. The decision to push the button has already been made by the brain in a way that is totally unconscious.

This whole experimental paradigm and the resulting discussions reveal the inadequacies of our current intellectual climate in which consciousness is routinely assumed to be of no importance. In fact, the discussions reveal not only bad philosophy but bad experimental design. All sorts of people who should have known better have said that the Libet experiments refute free will and show that our behavior is in fact determined. Perhaps free will is false, but Libet's experiments show nothing of the sort. A recent study[8] suggests the possibility that the experimental results are the result of requiring that the subjects stare at the clock. Maybe it is the clock that produces the readiness potential. If you conduct the same experiment where the subject decides *not* to move, the same "readiness potential" occurs.

The whole history of the discussion of the readiness potential, and the spectacular conclusions about the possibility of free will that were derived from it, reveal something very deep about the intellectual inadequacies about the present era. A large number of people who should have known better concluded from the Libet experiments that we do not have free will, that free will had been refuted.[9] But even on their own terms they show nothing of the sort. All they showed was that there was an increased activity in the supplementary motor area prior to the initiation of an action before the subject was aware of it. But it turns out that all of this is the result of the subject staring at a clock before deciding to perform an action. It would be interesting to go through all of the bad philosophy and bad neurobiology that was based on misunderstandings of the Libet experiments. I have

8. Trevena, Judy, and Jeff Miller. "Brain Preparation before a Voluntary Action: Evidence against Unconscious Movement Iinitiation," in *Consciousness and Cognition*,. 2009.

9. Koch, Christof. *Consciousness: Confessions of a Romantic Reductionist*. Cambridge, MA: MIT Press, 2012.

always insisted that even taken at their face value they show nothing about the impossibility of the freedom of the will.[10]

3. Reflexes

There are lots of anecdotal as well as scientifically substantiated cases where there is evidence for the initiation of action prior to conscious awareness. Anyone who has ever touched a hot stove will notice that he withdrew his hand before becoming aware of the heat. Any competent skier is aware that his body automatically adjusts to changes in the terrain before he is conscious of having moved his body. Spectacular examples are also given by professional athletes. The baseball batter confronted with a pitch coming at him at faster than ninety miles per hour has to begin his swing before he can become conscious of the oncoming ball. If his body waited for full consciousness of the ball, it would already be behind him. Similar examples are provided by tennis players who have to begin swinging at the incoming serve before they are conscious of it. Another famous sort of example is provided by experienced track runners who actually begin moving before they have consciously heard the firing of the starter's gun. The gun stimulates the brain in a way that initiates the runner's movement, but the actual processing in the auditory system is too slow for the runner to wait until he consciously hears the gun go off before he begins running.

In all of these cases, the subjects are unaware that they have begun a bodily movement before there is a conscious perception. How then do we know that they have in fact begun a bodily movement? The answer typically is that we know how long it takes the brain to process an incoming signal to produce consciousness. This could be as long

10. Searle, John R. "Can Information Theory Explain Consciousness?" *The New York Review of Books* 10 (January 2013).

as a half-second. But the trained body cannot wait that long, and so it starts moving prior to conscious perception.

These sorts of examples are just the tip of an iceberg of research that suggests that consciousness does not really matter much. On the Libet conception, consciousness *monitors* our behavior but does not actually initiate it. The initiation of the behavior is done unconsciously, and the conscious mind can then veto it but does not initiate it or carry it out. As Libet once said, we do not have "free will" but we have "free won't." Consciousness can veto an action that would otherwise have occurred.

Marc Jeannerod's book *Motor Cognition*[11] lends further support to the idea that much of what we think of naïvely as conscious mental processing is better explained by postulating unconscious mental processes that are actually carrying out the activity.

The picture that emerges around the time of this writing, the second decade of the twenty-first century, is that consciousness plays a genuine but rather minor role in human behavior. Much of our perceptual information is attained unconsciously, and many, perhaps most, of our actions are initiated unconsciously. Consciousness may function as a kind of policeman to guide our actions and may even veto certain sorts of actions, but the actual motor driving human cognition and behavior is unconscious. I think this view is totally mistaken and is not supported by the experimental evidence, and I will now explain why.

III. DOES CONSCIOUSNESS MATTER?

What are we to make of all these interesting data? Do they show that consciousness does not matter? Does the brain make up its mind to

---

11. Jeannerod, Marc. *Motor Cognition: What Actions Tell the Self.* Oxford: Oxford University Press, 2006.

do something before you are aware of having made up your mind? Do we conclude that you do not actually consciously see very much? Actually, I think they show nothing of the sort, and I will go through them one by one.

The most interesting case is the Deecke, Kornhuber, and Libet experiments on the readiness potential. Even if the experiments had been completely valid, the results would not have shown that free will does not exist. The subjects had already made up their minds to do something—in my jargon, they had formed a prior intention—but there was no suggestion that the situation prior to the action was in any way sufficient to cause the action. That is, there is no evidence that this refutes the freedom of the will, but of course the whole experimental apparatus was flawed by the fact that there were two variables: watching the clock and moving your hand.

It is clear that in our intellectual environment, a lot of people want to believe that free will does not exist and that consciousness does not matter much. I do not know whether free will exists, but I am convinced that consciousness matters enormously. Try to imagine me writing this book unconsciously, for example.

Several of the cases are reflexes. Notice that it is only the experienced baseball batter or tennis player who can start moving prior to any conscious decision, and I think it is obvious that something like a reflex is going on in these cases. I am an experienced skier, and I have this experience, very common in skiing, that my body will automatically adjust to changes in the terrain before I am aware of the change. My skis go over a bump, my knees automatically adjust, and I am aware of the bump and my reaction to it after they have occurred. The notion of a reflex is more complex than popular culture would make it out to be; but, all the same, in these cases there is something like a reflex in operation.

Again, the blindsight cases are interesting, but they are very marginal cases of perception. Nobody can drive a car, or for that matter write a book or watch a movie, using only the resources of blindsight.

Another common mistake is to suppose that because most of the processes by which we actually come, for example, to see something are themselves non-conscious neurobiological processes, that therefore there are unconscious mental processes going on in the brain that produce vision. This is a serious mistake which I have pointed out earlier. So, for example, research on the neurobiology of vision shows that there is a good deal of feedback from V1 (Visual Area 1) to the lateral geniculate nucleus (LGN). So a signal goes from LGN to V1, but then there is a good deal of feedback to LGN. The point that I am making is that though these processes are essential to the production of visual experience, there is no psychological reality whatever at this level. There is just a sequence of neuron firings without any mental reality at all. These are not cases of *unconscious mental processes*; these are cases of *non-conscious neurobiological* processes. And of course there are a very large number of non-conscious neurobiological processes in order that we should engage in any intelligent behavior at all. But it is a big mistake to see these as so to speak the tip of the iceberg of an unconscious mental reality that produces consciousness as sort of the frosting on the cake. To repeat a point I have made over and over: In order for something to be an unconscious mental phenomenon it has to be sort of thing that could be conscious, otherwise there is no psychological reality, no aspectual shape, no intentional content. And that is true of the non-conscious physiological processes that I have been citing.

The upshot of this discussion is that as far as we know anything at present about the operation of the brain and the operation of the mind, consciousness remains of absolutely central importance in any discussion of perception and of cognition generally. There are indeed shallow, unconscious mental processes, and these are often of serious importance, especially in questions of human motivation. But there is no such thing as the deep unconscious. There is, furthermore, a great deal of neurobiological processing going on in any perceptual experience, but this is not a candidate for mental reality, because it is all non-conscious. The feedback mechanisms of V1 and the LGN, for example, are crucial for the creation of conscious visual experiences, but they have no psychological reality. They create a psychology, but they are not themselves of any mental status; they are non-conscious rather than unconscious.

Chapter 8

Classical Theories of Perception

SKEPTICISM AND THE CLASSICAL THEORIES OF PERCEPTION

I said at the beginning of this book that perception was a central preoccupation of Western Philosophy since the seventeenth century. But most of the issues that I have discussed in the book were not the main concerns of the traditional authors on this subject. Their primary interest was epistemic: they were examining the evidentiary relation between the inner perceptual experience and the external world, where the investigation preceded on the assumption that only the inner perceptual experiences, the ideas or sense data, could be directly perceived. Specifically, given that all we can perceive are our own sense data, how is it possible to gain secure and certain knowledge of the external world? I have rejected the assumption that only sense data can be perceived. On the contrary, one thing that absolutely cannot be perceived is our inner perceptual experiences, our sense data. Once I have exposed the Bad Argument and gone into some detail about what an awful effect it had on the history of the subject, then I can discuss a series of questions which seem to me much more important than the traditional questions, and which the tradition cannot even address. That is, once you have accepted the Bad Argument, once you think that the objects of perception are always sense data, then the questions that I think are the interesting questions in the philosophy of perception cannot even be addressed. The

Disjunctivists make just as big a mistake as the tradition they think of themselves as opposing, because by accepting the formal structure of the Bad Argument and hoping to avoid its deleterious consequences by rejecting its first premise—the premise that says there is blank in common between the good case and the bad case, between the veridical case and the hallucinatory case—they make it impossible to address some of the really interesting issues about perception—for example, how the raw phenomenology sets intentional content, sets conditions of satisfaction.

In this chapter, I am going to address some of the traditional questions. Any general book on the philosophy of perception owes the reader some account of how the account relates to the problem of skepticism and how it relates to the traditional classical theories, such as the Representative Theory, Phenomenalism, Idealism, etc. Furthermore, at some point, the distinction between Primary and Secondary Qualities needs to be addressed, and I will conclude the chapter with a brief discussion of that issue.

I have to confess at the outset that I do not take many of these issues as seriously as many philosophers do, and that is one reason I have pushed them to the end of the book. I find it difficult to take skepticism seriously in any of its traditional forms. And once you have exposed the fallacy behind the Bad Argument and accepted an account of the intentionality of perception that justifies Direct Realism as a philosophy of perception, then many of the traditional disputes simply lose their interest. However, for the sake of completeness, here goes.

I. SKEPTICISM

Does the account of perception that I have provided in this book give any sort of an answer to skeptical doubts about the possibility of knowledge from perception? Skeptical arguments in philosophy in general (and indeed I think always) have the same form: no matter how much evidence (grounds, reason, warrant, foundation, etc.) you have for a claim, no matter how perfect your epistemic basis is for making the claim, you could always be mistaken. (Hume, the most extreme skeptic, argues that in fact you have no evidence.) There is always a gulf between the evidence and the conclusion. So you think you have evidence that the sun will rise in the east tomorrow (the problem of induction) or that other people are conscious (the problem of other minds) or you can know of the existence of objects by perceiving them (the problem of perception), but in every case you could have perfect evidence and still be wrong.

It is worth pointing out that there is a real problem in specifying exactly the nature of the putative epistemic base. Each of the terms I have used, "evidence," "reason," "warrant," "foundation," etc., can be misleading because each commits us to a certain way of looking at the matter. I am sure it is wrong to think that when I look at this table my visual experience is "evidence" that there is a table there. But what then is the right way to describe it? McDowell uses the expression "warrant," but that, because it is a legal metaphor, can be equally misleading. What is the exact right way to describe the relationship between my having this visual experience and my knowing that there is a table here? I think it is a form of identity. This visual experience just is a case of knowing that there is a table here. But that can be tricky, because I could have an experience exactly like this and not know that there is a table there. The phenomenology can be exactly the same in two cases, one of which is good, the other bad. That fact gives rise to skepticism.

Supposing this is the general form of the skeptical argument, does the account of perception I have given in this book answer it about perception? Well, in one sense it seems it does, because it says we do not have an evidentiary basis on which we make claims about objects in our vicinity. On the contrary, we directly see and touch objects around us. I do not have *evidence* that there is a desk there, I can *see* it. And seeing it is *knowing* it in this case. No more do I "have evidence" that there is a desk in front of me than I "have evidence" that I have two legs, I experience them directly. The big mistake is to think that seeing provides "evidence" (or ground or warrant or basis) it does not, and all of these are wrong. Seeing is the way of knowing.

So on a version of the skeptical argument that we have had now for several centuries, we do have a sort of answer to it. The skeptical argument says all you can ever perceive are your own experiences, so how do you know there is a reality on the other side of those experiences? On the account of perception that I have been presenting in these pages, the relation of perception is one of direct presentation. We do not have evidence or make an inference, we directly see objects and states of affairs around us. So the form of skepticism about perception that afflicted the classical philosophers—Descartes, Locke, Berkeley, Hume, Kant, etc.—does not afflict this account. In general, they had a choice between the Representative Theory, adopted by Locke and Descartes, which says you do not see objects but only representations of objects, or the Phenomenalism or Idealism of Berkeley and his successors. There, the problem of skepticism is removed, because there is no distinction between the evidence and the conclusion. The sense data that you see just are the objects that you see. This is a standard argument for Idealism in any form. The distinction between the evidence and reality is removed if the only reality is in fact the evidence.

Is my answer a satisfactory answer to skepticism? Well, in one sense obviously not, because it does not provide us any way to tell whether or not we are in an actual perceptual situation or whether we are having an indiscriminable hallucination. But the form of skepticism that we are left with is of a different dimension. It is not a question of never having enough evidence in principle; the question of evidence is removed altogether. I do not need any *evidence* that there is a table there, I can *see* it.

We might compare this answer to skepticism about perception of material objects to Wittgenstein's discussion of skepticism about other minds. Wittgenstein points out that we need to distinguish between "criteria" and "symptoms." If I see a man clutching his side and making a slight wincing facial movement, I might *infer* that he has a pain in his side. He is exhibiting the *symptoms* of having a pain. But if I see a man who has just been run over by a car and I can see his leg caught under the car and he is screaming in pain, then what I observe in this case are not symptoms of pain; but this, as Wittgenstein says, is a situation we *call* a man's being "in pain." Now, we might get it wrong in both cases. It might be in the symptoms case that the man was not in fact exhibiting pain, and it might be in the criteria case that the whole event was part of a Hollywood movie and they were just acting out a case of a man being in pain. But it is important in the second case to see that what is being acted out is precisely "man being in pain." That is to say, in this case, as Wittgenstein would put it, the language game of attributing pain is such that this is a case where it is legitimate to *call* it pain because the criteria are satisfied; and even in cases where we are mistaken, the mistaken attribution is, so to speak, founded on the very nature of pain.

This does not remove the possibility of skeptical doubt, but it enables to us to see the whole problem in a different light. The traditional skeptic about other minds wants us to think we do not have enough evidence, and Wittgenstein is saying if you distinguish clearly between *symptoms* (i.e., evidence) and *criteria*, you can see that the language game we play with the word "pain" precisely entitles us to use that word in the criterial case, even though there is nothing self-guaranteeing about the criteria. We might apply the word in the criterial case and still be mistaken for some reason, such as that there is acting going on. Now, applying that lesson to the case of seeing, just as we might say, "this is a case we call, 'a man being in pain,'" so we might say, "this is a case that we call, 'seeing a desk in front of me.'"

Of course I might be mistaken, but the dimension of the mistake is different from having an absence of evidence or insufficient evidence. So the upshot is that, assuming Wittgenstein is right about the case of pain and assuming I am right about the case of the perception of objects, in both cases it is still possible to raise a skeptical doubt. But the skeptical doubt is of a different dimension from that which the classical skeptic presents us with. It is not the absence of evidence or insufficient evidence, it is a different dimension of mistake altogether.

II. PHENOMENALISM, IDEALISM, AND THE REPRESENTATIVE THEORY OF PERCEPTION

One of the most fundamental distinctions among philosophers and types of philosophy, perhaps *the* most fundamental distinction, is in their answer to the question of what the philosopher regards as ontologically *rock bottom*. That is, for any philosopher who is willing to work out the implications of his philosophical position, there is an answer to the question, "What, if anything, is that in terms of which everything else has to be explained, but which does not itself have to be explained in terms of something else?"

On the account that I have been giving you in this book, it is clear that rock bottom is the world as described by atomic physics. This is not because I hold any special brief for a particular stage of the natural sciences; on the contrary, I assume they will continue to change and develop. But I do believe that, as a result of the past three hundred years of increase in knowledge, what we misleadingly call "scientific investigation," we can pretty well conclude that the known world is made up of entities that we find it convenient, if not entirely accurate, to call "physical particles." These particles exist in fields of force and are organized into systems, where the boundaries of the systems are set by causal relations. Examples of systems would be water molecules, babies, nation states, and galaxies.

I have to admit that I am embarrassed by dark matter and dark energy. On the other hand, my embarrassment is nothing like the embarrassment of physicists and cosmologists. When they say "dark," they are not talking about color but about their own ignorance. When I said "known world" above, I was deliberately excluding dark matter and dark energy. I have to let the physicists figure out the nature of these phenomena. But at any rate it is clear from the account that I am giving you that the account bottoms out in what I think of as the real world that exists in a way that is totally observer independent and ontologically objective. One of the tasks of philosophy is to explain the constitution of these higher-level systems and how they bottom out into the entities of atomic physics.

In the history of philosophy over the past three hundred years, the claim that ontology bottoms out in physics has not always been the dominant opinion. Indeed, the Bad Argument was so influential for so long that it led to two forms of the extension of the Bad Argument, both of which have ultimate reality bottoming out in subjectivity. One of these is the tradition of Idealism that says ultimately reality is ideal; that is, it consists of spiritual phenomena technically called "ideas." Physics, according to Hegel, is not the last word. On the contrary, physics is just a surface expression of something much more fundamental, the ontology of Geist. I think this Idealism survives in different forms in twentieth-century phenomenology, specifically in the work of Heidegger, Husserl, and Merleau-Ponty.[1]

Idealism comes in many different forms. I understand Berkeley's Idealism reasonably well. In our tradition of philosophy, we are all, in

---

1. Searle, John R. "The Phenomenological Illusion," in *Philosophy in a New Century: Selected Essays.* Cambridge: Cambridge University Press, 2008.

a sense, brought up on it. I do not understand Hegelian Idealism well enough to have an intelligent opinion about its details, but I think I understand it well enough in general to reject its idealist foundations. That is, the particular details of the form of Hegelian Idealism seem to me extremely obscure, but the rejection of physical particles as the rock bottom of ontology is, I think, very clear in German Idealism. I will have no more to say about it, because, as I said, I really do not understand it in detail.

Another tradition which has a completely different flavor on the surface, but which seems to me to commit exactly the same mistake, is the phenomenalist branch of the empiricist tradition. According to phenomenalist empiricism, exemplified by logical positivism, ultimately everything bottoms out in verification, where empirical verification consists in the perception of sense data. I think the positivists would have denied that on their view sense data was the rock bottom ontology. On the contrary, they would insist that they accept the ultimate ontology of atomic physics, but they would insist also that it is the task of the philosopher to clarify the *meanings* of these claims. And when you analyze the meaning of statements of atomic physics, or for that matter any empirical statement at all, it has to bottom out in sense data or it would be meaningless. On the positivists' account, the meaning of a statement is its method of verification, and empirical statements are verified by experience, that is, by sense data. I will say more about these issues later.

It is ironic that these two traditions, Idealism and Phenomenalism, though on the surface so different and ideologically opposed to each other, in fact, make the same mistake, and the mistake is based on the Bad Argument in both cases.

Another expression of the same underlying urge I have mentioned throughout is the Representative Theory of Perception. The criticism of the Representative Theory is relatively simple, so let us start with that.

III. REFUTATION OF THE REPRESENTATIVE THEORY OF PERCEPTION

According to the Representative Theory, we never actually perceive objects directly; rather, we perceive sense data, and we can get knowledge about objects from these sense data because in certain respects they resemble the objects that cause them. Representation comes by way of resemblance. So, when I look at the green table, the shape and size of the table are represented in my experience, and the table really does have shape and size. The resemblance between my sense data and the table itself enables me to get knowledge of the table from my experiences.

On the standard versions of the Representative Theory, as found for example in Descartes and Locke, not all of my experiences resemble actual features of the table. The color is a feature of my experience but not of the table itself. The table itself consists of colorless molecules. Traditionally, representative theorists distinguish between the Primary Qualities of size, shape, velocity, motion, and number on the one hand, and the Secondary Qualities of color, taste, sound, smell, on the other. The theory, according to Locke, is that the Secondary Qualities are not really qualities of the object but are just "powers" of the Primary Qualities to cause in us certain experiences. So on this theory, colors, for example, are a kind of systematic illusion. Objects are not really colored, but our nervous system is so structured that we have the illusion of color.

The decisive objection to the Representative Theory was already made by Berkeley when he said that ideas can only resemble other ideas. What he meant by that, in this context, is that the perceptual ideas that we have of an object could never resemble the object itself because the object is completely invisible and otherwise inaccessible to the senses. There is no way that the ideas we can perceive can resemble (or look like, or be visibly similar to) actual features of objects because the objects, by definition, are inaccessible to our senses. It is as if I said there were two cars in my garage that look exactly alike, except that one is totally invisible. The notion of "looking like" presupposes that both are visible, and on the Representative Theory one of them is not. Why does this matter? Because the form of representation in question requires resemblance. We are to think of the ideas as like pictures of the objects, but the picturing relation makes no sense if the object pictured is invisible. I think this is a decisive refutation of the Representative Theory, and I have never been able to take the theory seriously.

IV. REFUTATION OF PHENOMENALISM

Phenomenalism has such a long tradition, and it is so implausible, that it is hard for me to understand how so many brilliant philosophers could have taken it so seriously for so long. The idea is that all we perceive are sense data, but somehow that is all that there is to the world anyway, the actual sense data that we do perceive and the possible sense data that we could perceive. So on this account it is possible to say that there is a tree in the quadrangle even when no one is there to perceive it because if we did go into the quadrangle, we would perceive the relevant sense data. So the sense data need not be actual, they can be possible. In the heyday of linguistic philosophy, this was put in the "formal mode" by saying any statement about material objects, and indeed any empirical statement at all, can be translated into a statement or set of statements about sense data, and the statements can be both categorical (I am now seeing such-and-such sense data) or hypothetical (If I perform such-and-such operations I would perceive such-and-such sense data).

There are so many objections to this theory that one does not know where to start in refuting it, but the basic problem is that it reduces the public ontologically objective world to a set of private ontologically subjective phenomena. The aim of the philosophical analysis of perception is to analyze our ordinary and scientific sense of what it is to talk about perceiving objects and states of affairs in the world, and the phenomenalist-idealist analysis has the result that all such talk is really about ontological subjectivity. But that means that if the project was to account for our ordinary ways of thinking and talking, it fails. Well, what is wrong with saying that it fails, that all that exists are really private experiences in your mind and in other people's minds? The answer is that this results in solipsism. Now it turns out that the only phenomenon in the world that makes sense for me to talk about is my own experiences. If you have experiences, I could never know, because I could never experience them, and indeed, if you exist, you must be reducible to my experiences. (More about this later.)

There are standard textbook refutations of Phenomenalism. For the sake of completeness, I will later give brief summaries of some of the standard objections. However, I have to say that what bothers me about Phenomenalism and the Representative Theory is not some technical problem that they have, but their sheer preposterousness. They both have the consequence that you never actually see independently existing objects and states of affairs in the world; rather, all you can ever see are your own experiences. This is not because of some epistemic worry that we might have—maybe we are hallucinating, being deceived by evil demons, brains in vats, etc.—but rather because even if everything is going perfectly, all you ever see is your own experiences. Strictly speaking, you cannot even say that what you see is in the head, because of course the head is reducible to sets of experiences.

Before criticizing Phenomenalism, it is important to try to recover the enthusiasm with which it was accepted in the middle decades of the twentieth century. I have objected to it on the grounds that its fundamental ontology bottoms out in ontologically subjective sense data rather than the brute physical reality of atomic physics. This would have shocked the positivists themselves, and they would have objected to it. They thought reality bottomed out in physics, but they thought that the task of the philosopher is to explain what that *means*. And what it means has to be stated in a verificationist vocabulary because, according to them, the very meaning of a statement is given by its method of verification. The way you verify statements about physics is by perceiving the appropriate sense data. So it is not that there are two rival ontologies, the physical ontology and the sense data ontology. The fundamental physical ontology requires analysis into sense data in order to be meaningful. And what about my objection that this gives us a fundamental ontology which is, like Idealism, purely mental? The positivists would have said that all this talk about "fundamental ontology" is simply meaningless metaphysics. Their task is not to answer meaningless questions about the ultimate nature of reality, but rather to analyze the meaning of empirical claims. True claims about the world divide into two kinds, the empirical synthetic kind and the logical analytic kind. On the one hand, you have the sciences and most of ordinary common sense, and on the other hand, you have logic, mathematics, and tautologies; all else is meaningless. Now, of those two classes of claims, the empirical class, science and common sense, has a meaning which requires philosophical analysis in terms of sense data. The Phenomenalists prefer to put this point in the formal mode: Any empirical statement can be analyzed into sets of statements about sense data. They are equivalent in meaning. It might be that, in principle, the set of sense data statements would have to be infinitely long, but we can state the theoretical principles on which the statements are to be constructed, so no meaningless metaphysics is left over.

Now, how do I answer the positivists so construed? I think you cannot evade the charge of adopting subjectivist ontology just by converting to the linguistic or formal mode of speech. You have to ask yourself, What do these expressions in the linguistic formulations stand for? How does it all cash out? When you say any empirical statement can be analyzed into a set of statements about sense data, that must have the consequence that any empirical fact amounts to a lot of ontologically subjective facts about personal experiences, and these personal experiences always have to be in the minds of some individual human being. I do not see how the phenomenalist can avoid the charge that the doctrine is implicitly solipsistic. That seems to me the decisive objection to the phenomenalist analysis. The objective ontology of the real world is eliminated in favor of the subjective ontology of sense data. And because sense data are ontologically subjective, they are always in the minds of individual human subjects. But that means that I have no access to your sense data and you have no access to mine. If the meaning of a statement is its method of verification and the method of verification reduces all of my empirical statements to my experiences, then the meaning of those statements is solipsistic. Solipsism is a *reductio ad absurdum* of any theory. And this theory implies solipsism.

There were several technical objections to Phenomenalism, and I will discuss two of those. First, if you try to specify the antecedents of the conditional hypothetical statements that are supposed to provide the Phenomenalist analysis of the empirical statements, you will find you will always have to make reference to material objects; and thus the analysis does not succeed in reducing statements about material objects to statements about sense data. If the meaning of the statement, "There is a tree in the quadrangle that no one is looking at now" is to be given by the statement, "If we went into the quadrangle then we would see tree sense data," we have a problem because we had to make a reference to material objects in order to set up the hypothetical situation. We had to refer to our bodies and to the quadrangle and those are, so far, unanalyzed. A second objection is that it does not seem that you can get an adequate analysis, because it is possible to assert one side of the bi-conditional and deny the other side without contradicting yourself. It is always possible to say the sense data are there, but, all the same, there is no object; or to say that there is an object there, but, all the same, there are no sense data. Some Phenomenalists, in dealing with this difficulty, said that the set of statements that provided the Phenomenalist analysis might be infinite in number, but this did not seem an objection to them because precisely the notion of a material object might be, as John Stuart Mill suggested, the notion of an infinite set of possible sense experiences.

I will not go into much detail about these objections because, as I said earlier, the real objection is not some technical difficulty. The real objection is that the theory just seems to be inadequate to our own experiences. It is just a fact about our experiences that they reach right out to independently existing objects and states of affairs in the world. Furthermore, the object and state of affairs that they reach out to are in a publicly accessible world: You and I see exactly the same object. Neither of these claims can be accommodated within the phenomenalist tradition. On their view, all we ever see are sense data and sense data are essentially private.

One sees these difficulties in a striking form if you consider the conditions necessary for communication in a public language. How, on the Phenomenalist view, is it possible ever to communicate? How can we be saying something about a common world? The Phenomenalist thinks that a public language in which we can communicate to each other and in which our scientific truths are expressed, so to speak, comes for free. We can simply assume it and assume how it relates to our empiricist metaphysic. But I want to argue here that a public language presupposes a public world, and it looks like, in the denial of a public world, the phenomenalist has left us without a public language. Phenomenalists had various ways of dealing with this. At one point, Carnap said, strictly speaking, the *subjective content* of our utterances is incommunicable, but we can communicate a common *objective structure*. It is hard to see how this solves the difficulty. So, my objection to all of these theories based on the Bad Argument is that they leave us with essentially an unbelievable conception of our relation to the world.

V. THE CLASSICAL THEORIES AND THE PHILOSOPHICAL PROBLEM OF PERCEPTION

One of the most serious objections to the classical theories of perception, theories that are based on the conclusion of a Bad Argument, is that not only do they fail to give us a correct account of perception, they make it impossible to even pose one of the most important questions about perception. That question is: How is it that the specific features of the perceptual experience determine the conditions of satisfaction that they do? Now, why is it that the theories make it impossible to do that? The Representative Theory says that the way that the experience determines condition satisfaction is by resemblance. The resemblance between the perceptual experience and the object in the world enables the perceptual experience to represent the object. The perceptual experience is a kind of picture, an idea in the head, and that picture or idea actually resembles objects and states of affairs in the world. We have seen that no sense can be given to the notion of resemblance when one of the terms of the resembling relation is, by definition, invisible. So, the question is not adequately posed by the Representative Theory. The phenomenalist theory is even worse. In the phenomenalist theory there is not anything to the object except the sequence of our experiences. Objects just are "collections of ideas," as Berkeley put it. On the phenomenalist view any statement about an object, indeed any empirical statement at all, can be translated into a set of statements about sense data that, ontologically speaking, are subjective. There is no object on the other side of the sense data; the sense data is the bottom line of the analysis of objects. But all of these theories make it impossible to pose what I regard as the central question: How does the raw phenomenology of our experience set conditions of satisfaction such that the experiences are presentations of objects and states of affairs in the ontologically objective world?

VI. PRIMARY AND SECONDARY QUALITIES

A traditional distinction in the theory of perception is that between Primary and Secondary Qualities. The classic statement is in Locke's essay, though Locke did not invent the distinction. Primary Qualities are "utterly inseparable from the body in whatsoever estate it be." He says that these "Primary qualities of the objects themselves have the capacity to produce simple ideas in us, and these are solidity, extension, figure, motion or rest, and number." Secondary Qualities are "nothing in the objects themselves, but powers to produce various sensations in us by their primary qualities." He says these are "colors, sounds, taste, etc." Epistemically, the distinction is crucial for Locke because the ideas of Primary Qualities are actual resemblances. He says that:

> the ideas of primary qualities of bodies are resemblances of them, and their patterns do really exist in the bodies themselves; but the ideas produced in us by these secondary qualities have no resemblance of them at all. There is nothing like our ideas existing in the bodies themselves. They are, in the bodies we denominate from them, only a power to produce those sensations in us; and what is sweet, blue, or warm in idea, is but the certain bulk, figure, and motion of the insensible parts in the bodies themselves, which we call so.[2]

2. Locke, John. *An Essay Concerning Human Understanding*. London: Routledge, 1894. Book II, chapter 8, 87.

In the jargon that I introduced in the first chapter, on Locke's account, Primary Qualities are observer independent and Secondary Qualities are observer relative. They differ from the observer relative qualities that we have been discussing because they are not dependent on any activity of agents; unlike money and governments, they are not created by human intentional behavior. But, rather, the impact of the combination of Primary Qualities on our sense organs gives us the ideas of the Secondary Qualities.

It ought to make us a bit nervous that the authorities do not agree on a standard list, but it is not hard to construct a reasonable list. Primary Qualities are shape, the size of the mass (what Locke calls bulk), motion and number. By motion, he means whether or not the object is moving, and by number he means how many objects are there, one object or two objects, etc. The Secondary Qualities are easier to list. They include color, smell, sound, and taste. I think he should have also listed "texture," that is, the feel of the surface of an object, as a Secondary Quality. I think that this is a Secondary quality in Locke's sense, but he lists it as a Primary Quality.

Ontologically, it is an important distinction because it looks like there is a sense in which the Secondary Qualities are not real. They are, so to speak, systematic illusions created by the Primary Qualities. Objects are not really red or blue, but they have a combination of molecules that give us the impression that they are red or blue. So the attribution of redness and blueness can be epistemically objective, even though the colors themselves are observer relative. In Locke's jargon, the colors really are just the "powers" of the Primary Qualities to produce in us the experiences we call color experiences.

In recent years it has become fashionable to reject the distinction between the Primary and the Secondary Qualities, but I think there is something in it, and I want to spell it out. If you look at the lists of the Primary and Secondary Qualities, you notice several things. First, each Secondary Quality is from one sense only. Colors are from sight, sounds from hearing, odors from smell, and tastes from taste. The Primary Qualities are accessible at two senses and always the same two, sight and touch. For each of the traditional five senses, there is one, and only one, Secondary Quality, with the exception of the sense of touch. That is why I think texture ought to be listed as a Secondary Quality, though Locke does not so list it. Why is it important to be accessible to two senses? And the answer is that it is part of our concept of a material object that it has these Primary Qualities and that our basic dealings with material objects are based on a coordination of sight and touch. When Locke says that they are inseparable from the object in whatsoever state it might be, he is getting at this conceptual point. It is part of our concept of a material object—a chair, a table, a mountain, or a planet—that it should have the Primary Qualities, but it is not part of our concept of an object that it should have a certain smell or make a certain sound. You might think color is different because all material objects are colored. But even that does not seem to be part of a definition of a material object. Even though perfect transparency may be unattainable, you might still have an object that had no color because it was completely transparent. So there are some basic features of the distinction that survive criticisms. One is Locke's point that Primary Qualities seem to be essential to the concept of an object. And another, that the Primary Qualities are always accessible to the same two senses: sight and touch.

But what about the observer relativity of Secondary Qualities as opposed to the observer independence of the Primary Qualities? Well, if I am right in my account of how features of the world fix intentional content, then this distinction is not as sharp as we thought, because though red is partly defined as the ability to cause certain sorts of experience, being straight or being circular are also partly defined as the abilities to cause a certain sort of experiences. The dream of getting a one-to-one correlation between colors and certain wavelengths seems doomed to failure. Appropriate wavelengths are *sufficient* for producing the experience of red, but they do not appear to be *necessary*. All sorts of different wavelengths under appropriate conditions can cause the experience of red. But even granting the element of observer relativity in the basic perceptual features, there is still a contrast between the Primary and Secondary Qualities. One could put this point by saying that the basic geometry of the object figures essentially in its causal relations to other objects in a way that the Secondary Qualities do not figure in causal relations to other objects except by way of the Primary Qualities. The fact that this stone has this shape affects its causal relations to other objects. It will fit in certain places and it will not fit in others. The fact that this stone is red does not in that way figure in causal relations to other objects. One can object to this by saying that it does figure in causal relations: The fact that it is red will enable it to absorb light in a way that the fact that it is white would enable it to absorb less light. But to this objection one could say, in a Lockean vein, that the sheer physical reflectance properties can all be defined in terms of the Primary Qualities. The actual quality of color does not matter; what matters is the way that the object absorbs and reflects light waves.

My somewhat hesitant conclusion is that there is something to the distinction, but it is not quite what Locke had in mind.

NAME INDEX

SUBJECT INDEX